M
i

Peter Fleming & Max Amesbury

David Fulton Publishers

London

David Fulton Publishers Ltd
Ormond House, 26–27 Boswell Street, London WC1N 3JZ

www.fultonpublishers.co.uk

First Published in Great Britain by David Fulton Publishers 2001

Note: The right of Peter Fleming and Max Amesbury to be identified as the authors of this work has been asserted by them in accordance with the Copyright, Designs and Patents Act 1988.

British Library Cataloguing in Publication Data
A catalogue record for this book is available from the British Library

ISBN 1–85346–736–7

The publishers would like to thank Yvonne Messenger for copy-editing and Sheila Harding for proofreading this book.

Typeset by Mark Heslington, Scarborough, North Yorkshire
Printed in Great Britain by The Cromwell Press Ltd, Trowbridge, Wilts.

Contents

Preface

Teachers in primary schools are under pressure to continue to raise standards of pupil attainment by becoming ever more effective. It is now clear that middle managers have a pivotal role to play in this process. The DfEE and OFSTED alike have highlighted the key contribution effective middle managers can make in creating a 'can do' culture in schools and in ensuring quality practice at classroom level.

The skills required to be an effective middle manager in a primary school are many and varied but people management skills lie at the heart of getting the best out of both teachers and pupils. Motivating people and building a collaborative team ethos are at the core of effective management. This book is about how middle managers can contribute to raising the quality of education in their schools through proficient team leadership. In 1998 the Teacher Training Agency (TTA) published *National Standards for Subject Leaders*, underlining the importance being placed on middle management in the drive to improve achievement in schools. Generic skills highlighted in this document of value to all team leaders are covered in this book. A summary is provided as an appendix.

Using evidence from a range of sources, case studies and reflection on case studies the book will provide practical advice on:
- what it means to be a manager;
- the importance of vision and ethos;
- how to manage people and build your team;
- how to manage resources and administration;
- how to make meetings and communication effective;
- how to manage change and development;
- how to evaluate the performance of your team and set targets for teachers;
- how to avoid stress.

The book is intended for the three main groups of people listed below, though head teachers and deputies in primary schools, governors and those involved in teacher training and the provision of INSET may also find it useful.

1. **Newly appointed middle managers**

   For you the book aims to provide clear and practical advice to help you become effective and confident in your role. It will provide guidance on key aspects of middle management facing all team leaders, subject coordinators and year or Key Stage leaders. Through the use of case studies it highlights areas of potential difficulty for managers and in doing so should help you to avoid making major mistakes as you settle into your new post.

2. **Aspiring middle managers**

   The book will also be of value if you are seeking a middle management post. By introducing you to a range of situations and issues which might form the basis of questions used in the selection process it will help you to prepare for interviews with confidence. It is important to remember that good managers don't have all the answers but they do have a capacity for reflecting clearly on situations and they are able to make rational decisions on the basis of sound judgement. Reflections provided on case studies will help you to think effectively about a range of middle management issues.

3. **Existing middle managers**

   Successful managers remain open to innovation and change and they are continually reviewing their performance. This book grounds comments on effective management in evidence drawn from a range of sources. You will be able to use this evidence to evaluate your approach and consider ways in which you might improve the performance of your team. The emphasis on vision, leadership, and creating effective teams will be of particular interest to those who may have underestimated the importance of people skills in the past.

Acknowledgements

With thanks to the many dedicated primary teachers who have attended my management courses at Bradford College, and who have shared with me insights and reflections that have helped to inform the writing of this book.

Peter Fleming

Thank you to Eileen, my wife, for her willingness to proof-read and to check the content of my writing despite her own work commitments.

Max Amesbury

CHAPTER ONE

Introduction: What is Middle Management?

The term 'management' is relatively new to schools. It probably arrived with the introduction of local Management of Schools in the 1980s. Up to that point primary school head teachers had not seen themselves as managers and it is true to say that many are still not keen on that term being applied to them. However, it is probably fair to say that most primary schools today use the term senior management to describe one or more people whose responsibility it is to manage the affairs of the school. In a very small primary school this may be the head teacher while in a large primary it might comprise the Head, Deputy and Key Stage Coordinators (Foundation, Key Stage 1 and Key Stage 2). Some primary schools may consider that Governors are part of the management team and certainly OFSTED place great store on their managerial input. The rest of the members of the staff team, until very recently, would not have described themselves as managers. The growing use of the term subject manager led many primary school teachers, who may not have used the terminology before, to think of a middle layer of management.

It is surprising in many respects that the use of the term middle management has not occurred earlier in primary schools. After all, our secondary school colleagues have been using it for some time. The change from using separate terms for Head of Year, Head of Department, Key Stage Coordinator, Curriculum Coordinator to using a term with no specific group title occurred in the mid 1990s when the generic term *middle manager* was adopted. Management in general was seen by the DfEE and OFSTED as a key element in their drive to improve pupil achievement. Middle management, in particular, was seen as pivotal to improving our education system. 'Middle management has the power and responsibility to change systems and

1

reallocate resources to improve "best practice". Relating and cooperating in the pursuit of excellence are basic skills of the middle manager' (Trethowan 1991). Training for middle managers started to appear regularly on secondary school development/improvement plans.

While there are still some critics of the application of management theory and practice to education it is clear that a good understanding of management as applied to schools is necessary for any teacher interested in career advancement. More importantly, there is now plenty of evidence to suggest that effective school management is indeed helping to improve standards in schools and for this reason alone an understanding of what constitutes effective middle management is essential.

Defining middle management

Managers are people who can use available resources to accomplish a task or reach a target. It could be argued, therefore, that all teachers are managers. Certainly typical primary school teachers are involved in managing their teaching – lesson planning, delivery and assessment; managing pupils – their learning and behaviour; managing their classrooms – organisation and displays; managing their time and resources – teaching all the National Curriculum subjects and preparing the necessary teaching materials and equipment. These are all complex and demanding managerial tasks.

However, middle managers in schools are seen as those individuals who have additional responsibilities to those of the classroom teacher. They are a 'layer' of management between the senior management team and those at the chalk face. They play vital roles in planning for moving a school towards its goals, ensuring the smooth day-to-day operation of school business and monitoring the progress of others. In many schools middle managers provide the 'voice of reason', displaying a clear educational philosophy and idealism but also having their feet firmly on the ground because the bulk of their work is classroom based. Improving the quality of education for young people lies at the heart of school management and being able to motivate and organise individuals and teams to reach goals is essential, as the vast majority of middle management roles involve managing people. In an average-sized primary school with 240 pupils (one form intake with a Nursery) middle management jobs could include:
- Key Stage/Foundation Stage Coordinator
- Special Educational Needs Coordinator (SENCO)

- Staff Development Coordinator
- Planning, Assessment, Recording and Reporting (PARR) Coordinator
- Subject Coordinator.

The kind of questions asked at interviews for middle management posts are provided in Table 1.1 and help to clarify the nature of middle management in schools.

These questions illustrate that there are four major components of middle management:

1. Having a clear vision of the importance of the area for which you are responsible and being able to enthuse others with this vision. This is leadership.
2. Being clear about what constitutes good practice and using it. This is having specialist knowledge or know-how and being a good practitioner.
3. Being an effective manager of people and resources. It involves being able to plan, motivate, encourage good practice, challenge bad practice, solve problems and see tasks through. This is management.
4. Being able to put in place procedures to secure efficiency. This is administration.

Successful middle managers usually have, or very quickly develop, specialist knowledge relating to their roles. They then combine leadership, management and administration in the right proportions. Less effective middle managers may be good in one area but less successful in others. We can all call to mind coordinators who are

Subject coordinator	Key Stage coordinator
What unique learning experiences can your subject bring to young people?	What qualities does a good Key Stage coordinator possess?
What teaching strategies would you encourage your colleagues to use?	How would you deal with a member of your Key Stage team who constantly failed to hand in pupil data on time?
How would you deal with a member of staff who consistently did not complete the agreed programmes of study?	What kind of support would you offer to a member of your team who was struggling to maintain discipline in line with the agreement behaviour management policy?
What system would you like to see in place in order to track pupil progress in your subject area?	What kind of learning experiences would you like to provide for the children in your Key Stage?

Table 1.1 Interview questions for middle management posts

good administrators but fail to create any real vision for their team. Equally, some subject leaders can be charismatic and inspirational about their subjects but simply fail to put in place systems which result in good day-to-day organisation. Some posts will require more of one particular skill than another. At certain times the proportion of each skill needed to achieve results may change. Effective middle managers are sensitive to the need to develop their leadership, management and administration skills and are flexible in their application. Good managers are also honest about their weaknesses and will often successfully compensate for them by using the strengths of others in their team. It is reassuring to know that almost all the skills required to be an effective middle manager can be learnt, developed and improved. The art of middle management concerns judgement: the ability to assess a situation and the knack of combining management strategies in just the right proportions is what gives really good middle managers their flair.

The above analysis of middle management is evident in the Teacher Training Agency document *National Standards for Subject Leaders* (1998) which lists the following as key areas of subject leadership:

- strategic direction and development of the subject;
- teaching and learning;
- leading and managing staff;
- efficient and effective deployment of staff and resources.

Total quality management

Traditionally, particularly in the secondary sector, schools have operated a hierarchical model of organisation, based on the classical industrial model which is also evident in the armed forces and the church of earlier times. This model is best represented as a pyramid with the senior management team (SMT) at the apex, a layer of middle managers lower down and a broad base of standard scale classroom teachers (see Figure 1.1).

The pyramid is a rigid structure. Roles within it are clearly defined and everyone 'knows their place'. Job descriptions, formal meetings and institutional procedures serve to reinforce the structure. This model tends to hold back individual initiative with people strait-jacketed in their roles and can lead to an 'us and them' mentality. How many times have you heard such questions as, 'When are the SMT going to deal with . . .?' or 'That's for management to sort out – I'm paid to teach'. Most significantly of all, the clients of the school (pupils and parents) are not seen as important.

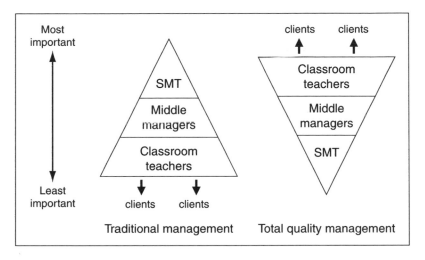

Figure 1.1 Traditional management and total quality management (TQM)

Management gurus, writing about management in industry and commerce, have argued for almost half a century for a less hierarchical approach. Peter Drucker (1990) advocated the empowerment of workers and Tom Peters (1991) highlighted the importance of companies creating learning cultures in which innovation is the norm and employees are focused on client satisfaction. In recent years these ideas have been refined into an approach known as *total quality management (TQM)*, which can be adapted to educational contexts. 'Total quality management is a philosophy with tools and processes for practical implementation aimed at achieving a culture of continuous improvement driven by all members of an organisation in order to satisfy and delight customers' (Marsh 1992).

In education the customer could be described as the pupil although it could be argued that parents are also customers. Primarily, however, schools exist to serve their pupils and in order to meet their needs a triangular partnership needs to be established between parents, staff and governors (Figure 1.2).

The interest from many schools and LEAs in the Pacific Institute's Investment in Excellence programme and the efforts by others to become 'Investors in People', or to gain the national 'Charter Mark' award, indicate the current interest being shown in management systems which value and empower all employees in their efforts to meet the needs of their clients.

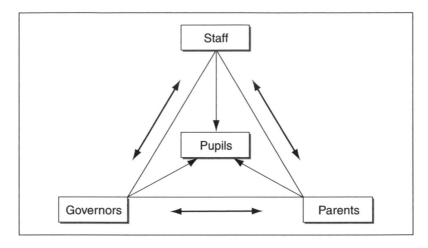

Figure 1.2 The triangular partnership

Total quality management is underpinned by the belief that an organisation (in our case the school) should be focused on client satisfaction and that there is always scope for improvement in the service being provided. A second element of TQM is the idea that every organisation has internal customers who also deserve a high quality service. Thus, in school, support staff provide a service to teaching staff and vice-versa. If a member of the support staff is struggling with an aspect of discipline then it is incumbent on the teacher to support that member of staff in order to maintain the school's standards on behaviour. Finally, TQM involves the effective use of data to measure performance and establish targets for improvement.

In schools that have embraced an approach based on TQM there is a clear focus on client needs. Senior management and middle managers see their roles, in part, as serving colleagues at the chalk face as effectively as possible to enable them to provide a high quality learning experience for their pupils. Hierarchies are less in evidence. Teams are more fluid. Leadership roles are encouraged on the basis of knowledge and skill rather than position in the hierarchy. For example, a young teacher with good Information and Communication Technology (ICT) skills could quite legitimately be encouraged to lead a working party investigating the use of ICT across the curriculum. They would be supported and assisted by more senior colleagues who would encourage a culture of collaboration. TQM schools systematically use data to provide evidence of how they are performing and are not frightened of asking probing questions about differences in performance between schools and teams within schools. At team level, similar questions are asked about differences in performance between teachers. This is not done to 'blame' particular teachers for poor performance but to establish reasons for under-performance and to address them.

Of course, this model can cause anxiety for teachers locked into the mentality of the rigid pyramid. Knowing 'where you stand' can provide a sense of security. Having to reflect on your performance can be threatening at first. However, there is now a wealth of evidence to suggest that schools with a traditional 'pyramid' form of management are ill equipped to cope smoothly with change and that, by contrast, a 'collegiate' approach produces dynamic and adaptable institutions (see Chapter 3). This approach does not remove the need for middle managers but it does require of them a particular frame of mind. They must be capable of:

- monitoring levels of client satisfaction and responding to client needs;
- using data to analyse performance and plan for improvement;
- motivating and empowering colleagues in their teams to perform to their maximum potential;
- clear thinking and creative problem solving.

It is likely that in the future these skills will become even more important, as the drive to improve school performance continues.

Good middle managers are not trapped in rigid strait-jackets but are flexible and adaptable, always on the lookout for ways to improve the education provided by their teams. They are able to move easily between roles – teacher, team leader, team member – as required. They gain satisfaction from empowering colleagues and seeing them succeed and constantly reflect on their own practice in the belief that better performance is always possible.

The context of middle management

Most medium to large primary schools will have a group of individuals whom they could label 'middle management' but it is likely they have not, as yet, been developed to their full potential.

The greatest barrier facing the development of an effective middle management layer in the primary school is associated with the history and tradition of this phase of education. Historically and traditionally the head teacher in a primary school has been expected to be involved in most, if not all, of the decision making. Although there has been a significant shift towards a more collegiate approach to decision making in recent years, primary school teachers still consider their role to be one of teaching and the head teacher's role one of management. Parents, staff, governors, the LEA, and OFSTED all expect the head teacher to be *au fait* with all that is happening in school and that nothing should happen on the decision front without the head teacher's blessing. This may be a reasonable expectation in a very small primary school but not one with, for example, 420 pupils (two form intake), 16 teaching staff and a variety of support staff totalling in the region of 30 individuals. The situation changed dramatically in primary schools during the 1990s and a change in the management structure (and each stakeholder's perceptions of that structure) is required in order to ensure that schools continue to move forward in the twenty-first century. However, it also needs to be recognised that a taxing management role in addition to the demanding role of teaching is one that many members of staff in the primary school, certainly in the short term, may not be rushing forward to develop. The climate and the culture have to be conducive for such change to take place and it is here that senior management has an important part to play.

The second historical factor which threatens the development of a middle management layer in primary schools is that of 'time', or rather the lack of it. The cry from all primary school teachers for many years is that non-contact time has been almost non existent. As the volume of paperwork increased during the late 1990s in line with government initiatives, the teacher unions challenged the Secretary of State for Education to reduce the bureaucracy with which teachers were faced. Part of the response by the unions and the DfEE was to suggest a reduction in meetings and to give that time back to teachers. Where this occurred, some schools found it adversely affected their attempts to increase their collegiate approach to decision making. Middle managers need time to do their job and it is not reasonable to assume that this can all be done after a busy day in the classroom. It is doubtful that many individuals, whether in industry or education, make their best decisions at the end of a difficult or demanding day.

So how can primary schools ensure that the conditions are right for the establishment of a middle management layer which can develop to its full potential? The answer lies with tackling the second historical problem first. Time needs to be created for middle managers to do their job, which in turn will allow them the opportunity to develop their managerial roles. After all, how can a subject leader monitor what is going on in a classroom without being provided with added non-contact time? How can a SENCO provide suitable advice for teaching and support staff without the opportunity to check on special needs children in their classroom environment? How can time be found for Key Stage Coordinators to meet? The new millennium and the change in government standard funding is now beginning to provide primary schools with the opportunity to develop a coherent and viable middle management structure. Primary schools are now in a position to buy in supply cover from outside without it impacting negatively on the school's budget. The cover can be used to release middle managers from the classroom on a planned and organised basis. Such a move is vital if schools are to provide middle managers with the opportunity to develop their roles.

Schools operate within particular localities and the local environment (geographical and social) is bound to influence the identity of the school. Likewise, schools are subject to national legislation and must operate within guidelines increasingly generated from central authorities. Most middle managers will have some responsibility for planning and monitoring the teaching of the National Curriculum and organising Standard Assessment Tests (SATs), for example. However, it is a fact that schools in similar areas can create different cultures and levels of performance, as data from OFSTED inspections indicate. Likewise, within the same school, some teams may exhibit very different cultures and it is now clear from 'value-added' data that a cohort of children can exhibit varying rates of achievement throughout their primary school career. The message here is that middle managers can make a significant difference, even in schools lacking strong senior management direction and support.

Schools that embrace a management style that encourages excellence, initiative and flexibility are likely to be well equipped to face the future and a *collegiate* approach will be advocated throughout this book.

Middle managers will be required to have knowledge and understanding of whole-school issues. Though they will 'fight their corner', good team leaders are able to take a wider perspective and should be supportive of the agreed school aims, especially those emphasised in the school's mission statement. In turn, good senior managers will involve middle managers and other colleagues in defining the mission and aims of the school so that there is a sense of ownership and clear direction.

Middle managers work in schools which have contact with many outside agencies and they will be expected to liaise with some of the following professionals:

- LEA officers;
- OFSTED inspectors;
- educational welfare officers;
- educational psychologists;
- initial teacher training tutors;
- LEA advisory consultants;
- university researchers;
- SATs assessment personnel;
- members of the police force;
- secondary school colleagues.

The ability to move easily into a range of situations or contexts is required. Dealing with fellow professionals will require the ability to adapt style and approach to suit the context. Written and spoken communication skills are important, with the ability to match language to audience. As well as meeting other education professionals, middle managers are likely to have dealings with a range of client groups – parents, local employers, journalists, etc. – and again effective communication skills are vital.

Middle management in practice

Being a middle manager does involve a variety of roles and wide-ranging tasks, but it does not mean 'being all things to all people' or never refusing to take on a commitment. To retain their sanity, teachers holding posts of responsibility must be clear about what is reasonable and what is not. This does not mean being petty about job descriptions, but it does mean being confident and assertive enough to draw the line when unreasonable requests are made. Ultimately, a stressed and over-worked middle manager will be ineffective and this is not what being a dedicated professional is about.

Middle managers are also teachers. Indeed, the bulk of their work is classroom based. Middle managers must consider their teaching role in the context of their management role. The values they hold as managers should be in harmony with the values they hold as teachers. If practitioner values and attitudes are transferable to management practice, teaching and management will coexist quite successfully. If they are not there could be problems. For example, an autocratic approach in the classroom is not a good idea but autocratic teachers might be able to survive. However, if they tried to run their teams as autocrats they would soon face rebellion. Likewise, coordinators and curriculum co-ordinators who promote differentiation at team meetings but don't apply differentiation in their own classroom will soon lose respect and credibility. This doesn't mean that middle managers must always be the best and most skilled teachers and good middle managers will acknowledge this. It does mean, however, that team leaders should set a good example in their practice and should not expect of colleagues what they cannot achieve themselves.

Key Stage co-ordination and subject co-ordination are common middle management roles. However, job descriptions provide a somewhat clinical statement of what a given middle management job entails. Knowing what is required in practice is the key to interpreting a job description successfully. It is essential for middle managers to identify their roles in terms of

- tasks;
- responsibilities;
- relationships (internal and external).

In order to do this they must be clear about the management and communication structures in operation in their school and be familiar with all school policies.

In practice, being an effective middle manager involves:

- *leading*, by being a role model for other staff;
- *serving* pupils, teachers and senior managers;
- *managing* the implementation of school and team aims and policies.

The art of getting the right balance can be elusive. Newly appointed middle managers often try so hard to serve that they neglect the managing dimension. In order to get things right, *critical reflection* is essential and the ability to reflect also equips middle managers to solve effectively the many problems and dilemmas they will face.

Middle management is not easy. In some schools team leaders can feel trapped between members of their team and senior management, as a result of conflicting expectations from these two groups of people. When teachers gain promotion internally to a middle management post, they take with them 'baggage' from their earlier roles and can sometimes find it quite stressful to settle into new relationships with colleagues. Sitting in any staff room and listening to conversations soon exposes team leaders who have not learnt the art of discretion. Professional integrity is very important for middle managers, as colleagues will trust and respect them only if they are certain that they can be approached in confidence.

Middle managers continually face role ambiguity and role conflict, with difficult choices to be made and, on occasions, difficult people to be confronted. How they approach such situations reflects on their integrity and often requires courage. Listening skills, sensitivity, reflection and persistence are all vital. The rewards of good middle management are visible in staff performance and pupil progress. It is also the case, in most schools, that good middle managers are respected and appreciated by junior and senior colleagues alike.

Middle managers are vital for the smooth running of a school. Responsibility posts can be exciting, rewarding and fulfilling. Hard working and professional team leaders can make a real difference in a school. They can bring a unique ethos to a team, transform lack-lustre subject delivery and make a significant difference to pupil performance. Newly appointed and enthusiastic Key Stage Coordinators and Subject Coordinators often find that they serve as a catalyst, allowing a team to shape or rediscover its commitment and enthusiasm. Most teachers are reasonable people who respond positively to good leadership and want the best for their pupils. Effective middle managers are aware that they are a vital part of the drive to improve standards in schools, and their motivation, at least in part, comes from a desire to do the best they can for their pupils. 'Throughout their work [a middle manager] ensures that practices improve the quality of education provided, meet the needs and aspirations of all pupils and raise standards of achievement in school' (TTA 1998).

Case studies

Below are two imaginary situations. Read each one and reflect on it from a management perspective. Think about the failures of middle (and senior) managers in these cases. How would you have dealt with each case? When you are clear about what you think read the reflections on the case studies.

Study 1

John Macdonald has had a wide and varied career and at the age of 45 considers he has found his 'niche'. Working in a 3–11 primary school he has a Year 5 class, which he considers to be his favourite year group. On the one hand they are old enough to 'work on their own' without placing too many demands on him. On the other hand they are still full of enthusiasm and don't provide him with the problems that the 'top dog' Year 6 children used to give him. John is second in command in the science department (with no allowance) but with particular responsibility for upper Key Stage 2 (Years 5 and 6). His apparent lack of enthusiasm for his job in general has led the school's Science Coordinator to use John merely as a sounding board for her own ideas. John's last appraisal, however, indicated that he was a talented science teacher who displayed some interesting approaches to teaching the subject. His record keeping on pupil achievement left much to be desired and he was often late handing in pupil record cards to the Key Stage Coordinator.

What should the school's middle managers be planning to do with John? Are they getting the best from him? What would you do?

Reflection

Should the Key Stage 2 Coordinator consider suggesting to Senior Management that John needs a change of year group in the not too distant future, in case he becomes 'too comfortable' or complacent? Was the Science Coordinator involved in the last appraisal? If no, should she have been? If yes, should she not be looking to use his talents to improve science teaching across the school? Could his self-esteem and his enthusiasm in general be improved if he was involved in leading others? What kind of support should the Key Stage Coordinator provide in order to improve John's approach to record keeping?

Study 2

Ben, a Year 3 pupil, was giving problems at lunchtime. He wouldn't do as he was told by the lunchtime assistants and he seemed to spend most of his time falling out with members of his own class. Ben had special needs and although he could be awkward from time to time his behaviour towards the end of October was unusual.

The lunchtime supervisor reported Ben's behaviour to the class teacher, Larry Marr, who replied he would have a word with the boy but added that what happened at lunchtime was outside his jurisdiction.

Ben's poor behaviour continued and the lunchtime supervisor decided to have a word with the school's SENCO. The SENCO decided to approach Larry personally but received a caustic retort from him stating that the boy concerned was a problem in and out of the class and that this type of pupil should not be in a main stream school. The SENCO discussed the situation with the Ben's Special Needs Assistant

(SNA) who informed her that Ben sits on his own in the classroom and that she as his SNA is expected by Mr Marr to have total responsibility for Ben's Individual Education Programme (IEP). The SNA considered that the main reason for Ben's behaviour at lunchtime was due to his general dissatisfaction with the classroom situation. She said it had been getting steadily worse for some time but didn't feel it was her place to say anything as she had to work with Mr Marr each day.

Where have the SENCO and the Staff Development Coordinator gone wrong? What would you have done?

Reflection

Had Larry Marr had any training for working with Special Needs children? With more and more children with *very* special needs being included in main stream education, should the SENCO and Staff Development Coordinator be suggesting to Senior Management that 'inclusion training' should be a staff development priority? Should the SENCO make it part of her responsibilities to check early in the school year with her support staff and teaching staff that they are happy with the Special Needs situation in their classroom? Should the SENCO make a point of liaising more closely with the lunchtime staff, who are obviously struggling to deal with the more demanding children in their charge?

There are other points to pick up from this case study:

- Ben has been treated badly. He will feel resentful towards the school. He may involve his parents. This may create the need to involve a senior member of staff. If the parents feel badly treated they will speak ill of the school to their friends and neighbours and this may influence whether or not they send their children to the school. Worse still, Ben is an unhappy pupil and the school is failing him. He may decide to attend a different school.
- In this case, ineffective middle management could result in the school losing pupils and the revenue they bring with them.
- It is important that relatively minor concerns are recognised and dealt with at an early stage before they develop and escalate into major problems.
- Although it can be argued that staff need an uninterrupted lunchtime, can problems which occur during that period involving children in their care be ignored? Certainly in the short term, the repercussions can adversely affect the afternoon teaching session,

while in the longer term staff teamwork can suffer, as can overall school discipline.

Summary

Over the past twenty years management theory and practice has been adapted and applied to the education system, with the aim of improving the achievement of young people and making schools more accountable. There is clear evidence that better management is helping to improve standards in schools and for this reason there is currently a drive towards enhancing the management skills of middle management in schools.

Schools taking a collegiate approach to management operate flexibly, empowering teachers to be creative (but also accountable) and use their skills and talents to improve the education of the young people they serve. Such schools have a clear client focus and encourage collective responsibility. When things go wrong blame is shared and people work together to find solutions. Such schools are proving to be better at coping with change than more rigid, hierarchical organisations.

Middle managers in schools are concerned with creating a clear sense of purpose for their department or year group; managing teams of people, individuals and other resources effectively to achieve agreed targets; and ensuring that routine administration is efficient and effective. In schools where total quality management or a similar philosophy is being encouraged middle managers are engaged in developing a clear client focus and in ensuring that internal customers, as well as pupils, parents and other client groups, are provided with a good quality of service.

Middle managers play many roles and need to be able to adapt comfortably to each role. As teachers, team leaders and team members they need to behave appropriately and display a level of commitment and integrity deserving of respect. Middle managers lead by example; they are active in helping to shape the school's mission while at the same time being sensitive to the pressures faced by classroom teachers. Good middle managers develop clear reflective thinking as a means of solving problems they encounter and to help them to be more proactive in the shaping of events.

All middle managers face challenges, demands, dilemmas, and obstacles. At times they can feel frustrated and even demoralised but it is also the case that middle management can be exciting, challenging, rewarding and fulfilling. Middle managers who help a team develop a clear identity and group loyalty foster a sense of purpose and make a real difference in the quality of education provided.

Commitment and effort with which middle managers approach the challenges of their post can usually be equated with the degree of job satisfaction.

CHAPTER TWO

Different Management Styles

Introduction

While it is obvious that all human beings are unique individuals, it is also true that certain traits common to large numbers of people make it possible to group similar individuals together and predict their behaviour. Social scientists have studied common traits and the predictability of behaviour in order to classify people according to personality, social class, cultural group and so on. It is now generally felt that the behaviour we observe in individuals is a product of genetic make-up, social learning, and the contexts in which individuals operate. This is as true for managers as it is for any other social group.

When listening to middle managers talking about how they approach their work, it is possible to fit them into particular categories, according to their predominant management style. Likewise, when working with teachers aspiring to middle management posts, the introduction of models of management style into a teaching session usually results in an immediate acknowledgement of the usefulness of management theory. This is because teachers can instantly recognise in the models the managers they work with, and this seems to assist them in understanding the reasons for the success or lack of success of the managers they know.

It is useful to analyse the various styles of management uncovered by management theorists and reflect on their utility in the primary school context. Before doing this, however, it is important to consider the following points:

- Management style is not fixed. While certain personalities are more likely to approach the management of others in a particular way, everyone can learn new ways of managing people. The important thing is to be open-minded and self-critical. Some may be predisposed to a particular style of management, but if there is clear evidence that other styles seem to be more effective then the good manager will learn to use the features of the style that is known to work.

- Different situations require different management styles. Good managers are able to adjust their approach to suit the task, the context and the individuals with whom they are working. Even when there is evidence that a particular style of management is *usually* effective, there may well be circumstances in which other styles are needed to produce the required results. Being able to assess which situation requires which style is critical.

- Middle managers work in teams. By knowing the personalities of your team you will be able to use the skills of others to complement your style of management. Again, this requires honesty and critical reflection. Don't be afraid to use the strengths of others; knowing more about management styles will help you to assess yourself and see how others in your team can be used to complement your particular strengths. Skilled managers make this look easy, but it is something young managers often struggle with, believing, wrongly, that they should be capable of being all things to all people. A degree of humility, coupled to the ability to make others feel valued for their particular strengths, is what makes many team leaders in primary schools successful.

Models of management

Research on management styles has identified clear traits and management theorists have assembled these traits into typologies of management style and management models. A number of these models are identified in this chapter. Some of the models, naturally, have similarities, and a synthesis of them can help in reaching a clear understanding of the key characteristics of managers you know and of yourself as a manager.

The authoritarian/laissez-faire axis

One simple model of management places all managers somewhere on a continuum from *authoritarian* to *laissez-faire*, with most managers showing traits that place them in one of the following groups:

Authoritarian ⟶ **Democratic** ⟶ **Laissez-faire**

The groups are based on an analysis of how managers behave towards the people who work in their teams. At one end of the scale are authoritarian managers (dictators who need to control all aspects of a team's work); at the other end of the scale are laissez-faire managers (who seem happy to allow colleagues to do just as they please). In the middle are democratic managers who share a clear sense of purpose with team members and involve colleagues in deciding the most appropriate ways of achieving agreed goals.

Most managers, if honest, will admit that their approach resembles one of these positions. Certainly, people working in their teams rarely have any difficulty in identifying their style of management as the characteristics displayed are easy to identify (see Table 2.1).

The MacGregor X-Y axis

While the laissez-faire approach amounts to a failure to manage, the authoritarian and democratic typologies seem to reflect conflicting underlying assumptions about human nature and how people should be treated in order to get the most out of them in a work situation. The American management consultant, Douglas MacGregor, first identified two extreme and opposing sets of beliefs held by managers in his book *The Human Side of Enterprise* (1960). MacGregor's categories are given in Table 2.2.

Authoritarian	Democratic	Laissez-faire
• Tells people what to do • Keeps information from team members • Stifles debate • Tightly controls meetings • Gives the impression that decisions are made before they are discussed • Employs rigid procedures • Seems to have 'tunnel vision' • Fails to develop colleagues by refusing to delegate	• Directs or supports people as necessary • Shares information of relevance to the team • Plans well-structured meetings which allow for debate but reach decisions • Agrees clear procedures with the team • Has a clear philosophy but listens to other views • Develops colleagues by negotiating the delegation of some tasks	• Doesn't like directing people • Shares information unnecessarily • Allows so much debate clear decisions are rarely made • Allows meetings to drag-on • Lacks procedures • Gives the impression of having no clear philosophy for the team • Fails to develop colleagues by not planning delegation

Table 2.1 Authoritarian, democratic and laissez-faire managers

MacGregor X thinking	MacGregor Y thinking
• People are naturally lazy • People are not interested in improving their performance • People need supervision • People can't be trusted with making decisions	• People are naturally motivated • People want to do well and improve their performance • People want to take responsibility • People thrive on being involved in decision making

Table 2.2 MacGregor X and Y thinking

Newtonian and Whiteheadian managers

There are echoes of the MacGregor axis in the more recent materials developed by the Pacific Institute for their Investment in Excellence programme, now being widely applied in education and other public service organisations. According to Louis Tice (Pacific Institute 1997), people can be classed as either Newtonian or Whiteheadian, depending on how they see the world. These views of the world can have a profound influence on the way they manage others.

Isaac Newton, in the seventeenth century, was deeply interested in religion. Through his scientific work he wanted to show the order which existed in God's universe. He believed that the world was entirely predictable except for human beings, who represented a threat to God's creation. Therefore, according to Newtonian logic, human beings must be controlled. In organisational terms this means people must know their place, must have rigid procedures to follow and must not be given the autonomy to take risks. Managers are there to keep people on-task and prevent them working against their employers and disrupting the smooth running of the organisation.

Alfred North Whitehead (1861–1947) was a mathematical physicist and a philosopher whose world-view was very different. In contrast to Newton, he believed that God was working to make a better world. Far from being a threat to God's ordered world, human beings were, in fact, capable of inventing better ways of doing things; they were helping to move the world towards perfection. Applied to organisations, a Whiteheadian approach results in people having more autonomy, with accountability spread throughout the organisation. The job of management is to empower people creatively to achieve the goals of the organisation. Far from being seen as a threat, the workers are seen as the key resource of an organisation.

During the last twenty years more and more organisations, including public service industries, have embraced the Whiteheadian

Newtonian managers	Whiteheadian managers
• Assume a basically stable environment • Assume people are basically lazy and incompetent • Think control must come from above • Think only managers are accountable • Get self-esteem from power and position • Think people work best when given set tasks	• Assume constant change • Believe people can be creative and inventive • Think control should be shared • Think accountability should be shared • Get self-esteem from supporting and nurturing others • Think flexible people are more useful

Table 2.3 Newtonian and Whiteheadian managers

perspective. Through initiatives such as 'Investors in People' the importance of developing individual potential so that people can contribute to the organisation has been acknowledged. Research into school effectiveness has demonstrated the benefits of involving all staff in planning and decision making and encouraging both greater autonomy and accountability. Put simply, schools taking a Whiteheadian approach to management seem to be more dynamic and successful. Middle managers, therefore, would be advised to take such an approach with their teams, though this is clearly more difficult for team leaders working in Newtonian schools. Whiteheadian middle managers working in Newtonian schools would need gradually to change the culture of their teams, as Newtonian team members are likely to be over-dependent on their managers. These themes will be expanded in Chapter 3 when effective cultures are explored.

Task-orientated managers and people-orientated managers

Another way of classifying managers is to place them on a continuum somewhere between the extremes of *people-orientated* and *task-orientated*.

People orientated ——▶ Task orientated

Managers who are strongly task-orientated tend to be good at planning and administration. They are often efficient and can be relied on to 'get the job done'. However, the downside of being strongly task-orientated is a tendency to lack tolerance for those who are unable to work as efficiently as the team leader and a frustration with those who challenge plans being put into action. Task-orientated managers are often seen as aloof and can sometimes fail to consult colleagues, being over-zealous about 'getting on with it'.

In contrast, people-orientated managers tend to be less bothered about planning and administrative efficiency and more concerned with keeping up the morale of people in their team. They are usually prepared to devote a great deal of time to listening and feel that consulting colleagues is an essential aspect of management. Strongly people-orientated managers can spend so much time on 'keeping people happy' that they neglect to move their team forward towards achieving agreed goals.

A successful manager is someone who can combine a concern for people with administrative efficiency and the ability to get things done. In reality, most middle managers fall somewhere between the two extremes mentioned, and it is certainly possible for managers with a tendency to one extreme or the other to compensate for this by conscious effort based on critical reflection and the learning of new skills.

There are similarities between the people/task continuum and the authoritarian/laissez-faire axis. Managers who fail to consult and are obsessed with administrative systems are sure to be seen as authoritarian by colleagues. Likewise, managers who are so concerned about the different views and feelings of colleagues that they are never able to lead a team to a consensus or a clear decision end up, even if unintentionally, being laissez-faire managers.

Figure 2.1 illustrates the links between some of the management characteristics mentioned earlier in the chapter and the people/task classification.

1. Position A managers are strong on people but weak on task. They are fair and considerate to people, trusting them to be professional and get on with their jobs. Such managers may, however, fail to give a clear sense of direction and may also fail to develop the skills and potential of those in their team. With a highly motivated and highly skilled team, in a fairly stable organisation, it is possible for *people managers* of this type to be successful.

2. Position B managers are efficient and well organised, with a clear sense of what needs to be done to move their team forward. However, it is likely that such managers do not adequately involve colleagues in deciding on goals or ways of achieving them. B managers may be irritated by people in the team who do not share or understand the goals, and are unlikely to be sympathetic to people slowing down the process of change. In rigid, hierarchical organisations there are plenty of these *authoritarian managers*. Arguably, such people can be useful as

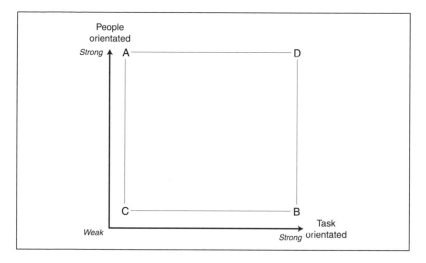

Figure 2.1 People-orientated and task-orientated combinations

middle managers in schools, when particular tasks need accomplishing quickly and efficiently. However, schools are people-orientated organisations that largely depend on teams working together and individuals being nurtured to perform to the best of their ability. For this reason B managers may have limitations in some situations.

3. Position C managers are weak on both task and people skills and, as such, fail to manage at all. C managers are *laissez-faire managers* of the worst kind, being unable to get tasks done but also leaving colleagues to their own devices with no concern or support being offered. In most schools, thankfully, laissez-faire managers are becoming extinct, as the pressure of constant change, greater accountability and regular inspection makes it impossible for such individuals to survive.

4. Position D managers are able to combine the ability to accomplish tasks with a genuine concern for colleagues. Such managers have clear goals and clear ideas about how to move towards those goals. In addition, D managers are capable of engaging other team members in deciding how goals can be achieved and are supportive of colleagues who encounter difficulties with change. D managers are good listeners, make effective use of the skills of people in their team and are flexible. Above all else, D managers are able to keep the morale of the team high and, by so doing, enable the team to reach agreed goals.

D managers would obviously make outstanding primary school leaders and we would encourage middle managers in primary schools to aim to become D managers. However, we are very conscious that no manager can be 'all things to all people', and in the primary schools of today the pace of change and the demands from above mean that it is simply impossible to be perfect textbook managers at all times. Primary middle managers, usually managing a team of people in addition to teaching a class on a full time basis, should not, therefore, feel inadequate if they fall short of being D managers on all occasions.

Management styles and fitness for purpose?

The problem with looking at models of management style is that they distort reality. While most managers display traits which make it easy to place them in a particular category, it is likely that most authoritarian managers have some people skills and most people-orientated managers have some planning ability and an awareness of tasks to be done. The important thing is that managers are realistic and honest about their strengths and weaknesses as a starting point for improving management performance.

Peter Fleming well recalls a management training session with a group of middle and senior managers from the same school which illustrates this point. When the course members were working in small groups on management styles, it soon became clear to him that just about all the middle managers had identified one member of their senior management team as a textbook example of an authoritarian manager. This senior manager was present at the training session and was telling members of the group he was working with how well he thought he fitted the democratic model of management.

The massive gap between the assessment made by his colleagues and the self-assessment of this particular manager rang alarm bells for Peter. There was potential for friction in the school concerned arising from the contrasting views of his behaviour. It is important that managers are genuinely self-critical and make themselves aware of how they are seen by others. Armed with this knowledge, it is possible to begin working on areas of weakness in order to become better and more rounded managers. Adair (1997) sums up the importance of understanding how others perceive you rather amusingly as follows:

If one person says that you are a horse,
Smile at them.

If two people say that you are a horse,
Give it some thought.
If three people say that you are a horse,
Go out and buy a saddle.

It is also vital to realise that using a style of management *fit for purpose* is also very important. When the school fire bell rings it is essential that even managers who are highly people-orientated snap into an authoritarian mode, for everybody's sake. Having a meeting to ascertain how people feel about evacuating the building would clearly be ludicrous. More serious examples are easy to find. Newly appointed middle managers facing an OFSTED inspection, and needing to get various things in place, might need to use a task-orientated style, even though they might be committed to a more democratic approach in the long run.

Different styles of management may also be needed for different people. While a democratic, people-friendly approach may be the most effective style of management for colleagues who are committed and professional, a more authoritarian style may have to be used with colleagues who are uncooperative and deliberately obstructive, if all else fails. Depending on the level of skill of people in a team, managers may find themselves *directing*, *coaching*, *supporting* or *delegating* in order to get the best out of each individual. This theme will be explored in Chapter 4.

Just as good middle managers make effective use of the strengths of individuals in their team, so good senior managers will be aware of, and use appropriately, the strengths of their middle managers. In one primary school the review of the school's approach to Equal Opportunities was delegated to a middle manager with strong people skills, rather than being led by the head teacher. She was able to create the right sort of ethos in meetings, which allowed for very different views to be expressed openly and debated in a non-threatening way. This example shows the importance of using people's strengths and ensuring *fitness for purpose,* with the aim of creating an organisation that effectively meets the needs of all the people within it. 'Effective management is about working with and through others in order to maximise impact where it most benefits all pupils. It is about enabling things to happen, empowering colleagues and helping to establish the necessary conditions' (West 1997).

Case study

The Key Stage Coordinators at Leafy Glades Primary School were asked by their head teacher to work with the staff in their two Key Stages on a review of the school's homework policy. Did staff consider any changes needed to be made? If 'yes' what changes were required? Ideally, a consensus should be achieved and a statement for the Key Stage 1 and Key Stage 2 sections of the homework policy produced.

The Key Stage 2 Coordinator, Janet Barton, knew that achieving a consensus would be difficult as the issue was considered somewhat controversial by a number of the teachers in the upper end of the school. Consequently, she decided an autocratic approach was appropriate in this instance. Using the guidelines on homework provided by the DfEE, Janet suggested to colleagues that they had no real alternative but to accept the guidelines and that the school's policy should be altered accordingly. Considering that discussion was a waste of time teachers in Key Stage 2 grudgingly accepted Janet's suggestion.

Consequently, she was able to supply the head teacher with a 'decision' and a statement on homework in Key Stage 2 within a few days of being set the task.

The Key Stage 1 Coordinator, Peter Mansi, arranged to meet with colleagues to discuss the school's homework policy, suggesting it should be the only item on the agenda. The meeting, which lasted an hour, involved all the staff in frank and open discussions.

Unfortunately, no consensus was reached and it was decided staff should go away and think about what had been said. Another meeting was scheduled for the following week. It was obvious by the time the second meeting occurred that much discussion had taken place between staff in the interim. Nevertheless, it still took an hour of debate before a consensus was achieved. There was a further delay while the homework statement was written and then distributed to staff for their approval before it finally finished up on the head teacher's desk.

When both statements were read by the head teacher, it was apparent to her that they were different in tenor and did not sit comfortably alongside each other. Consequently, it took a further meeting between the Head, Deputy Head, Janet Barton and Peter Mansi to produce a homework policy which appeared 'consistent' in its approach. In order to achieve this situation both Key Stage Coordinators had to compromise.

This new version was then put before the whole staff. Key Stage 1 staff did not accept at first all the suggested changes to their part of the document. However, following discussions, they did agree to some minor alterations. Key Stage 2 staff, on the other hand, accepted their altered statement without argument, giving the impression that they lacked interest in the whole procedure.

Parents and governors were asked for their views on the policy and apart from a few minor alterations, which were accepted by the staff, the homework policy was adopted.

Within a period of six months, however, it became apparent that the policy was not 'working' at Key Stage 2. Homework was not being applied consistently and there was grumbling among the staff. Matters came to a head at the next Key Stage 2 meeting where a number of staff aired their views over the process leading up to the Key Stage 2 homework policy statement. They had not been consulted nor had they had a chance to offer their suggestions. They felt they had been given no choice but to accept the DfEE guidelines *per se*. Their considered opinion now was that a new review of the Key Stage 2 section of the homework policy should take place as soon as possible.

Reflection

Janet Barton learnt through this experience that an autocratic approach to management doesn't always work. Dictating to a team may work if the decisions made have a minimal impact on others. However, as in this case, if others are to play a large part in ensuring the policy works, they need to be involved in the decision making process and, ideally, a consensus should be achieved before the policy is put into practice. Ensuring that team members feel 'ownership' of school policies is a key aspect of middle management and is best achieved by managers who favour a democratic approach.

Reflect on your own experiences as a teacher. Can you think of team leaders or managers you have known who fit any of the models discussed in this chapter? Are there traits from any of the models you recognise in your own approach to management? When you have been involved in policy making, what strategies have managers used to encourage your commitment and to help you feel 'ownership' of the policy? Did these work? Why or why not? Can you think of any situations in which a leader might be justified in adopting an authoritarian approach to team members?

Summary

A number of different management styles have been identified and these styles are easily recognisable in school contexts. Some managers have a tendency towards being *authoritarian* and *task-orientated* while others seem to be more *people-centred*. The most successful managers are those who can combine effective planning for the achievement of clear goals, with a style of managing people that is supportive and motivating. This is especially important for middle managers in schools, who regularly find themselves having to lead their teams towards goals set externally by senior managers or central authorities.

Generally, a style of management that involves others in decision making and empowers individuals to use their talents to achieve goals is most effective. However, different styles of management are appropriate for different tasks and in different contexts. Good managers will be flexible about the styles they use and will learn to slip between styles depending on the task they are undertaking and the people they are dealing with. Thus, the ability to reflect and analyse is very important for managers who want to ensure that the approach they use is *fit for purpose*.

Managers operate in the way they do because of a combination of personality, training, institutional culture and immediate context. All managers are capable of learning new skills and it is possible for determined managers to enhance their performance. To do this, though, they must be open, honest and self-critical. They must involve others in appraising their performance so that they begin to see themselves as others see them. Only then will they be able to improve those aspects of their management activity which need development.

Good managers see it as a duty to develop the skills of people in the teams they lead. By using the abilities of others, effective managers can often compensate for weaknesses they acknowledge in themselves. Middle managers should not feel threatened by others in their teams who have skills and attributes they lack, but should see these people as a rich human resource to be used to the benefit of the school and the children in the school. Managers who are unsure of their own abilities often find humility difficult. Those who are confident about their strengths and aware of their relative weaknesses will often have less difficulty in helping others shine and develop.

CHAPTER THREE

A Look at Effective School Cultures

Introduction

Those readers who have the opportunity to visit many schools will be aware of just how different schools with comparable intakes of pupils can be. It would be easy to assume that schools in similar areas would be very much the same, given that they all have to deliver the National Curriculum and that they serve similar parents and cater for similar types of pupils. This is simply not the case: on walking into some schools the positive ethos is palpable, whereas in others a very different atmosphere exists. This is not simply a matter of the appearance of the buildings or the layout of the reception area, it is about the culture that the organisation has developed and lives by.

When you enter a school and feel a positive ethos and sense a real culture of cooperation and achievement you can be sure that this doesn't exist by accident. It is likely to be the result of a vision shared by all staff, good selection and training procedures, and effective policies which give staff and pupils a clear sense of direction, together with considerable autonomy and responsibility. It is likely that in these schools staff have high expectations of the children and one another and that there is a strong belief in involving pupils in decisions about their learning. These schools have usually embraced some aspects of a total quality management approach (see Chapter 1), especially the importance of believing that both internal and external clients are deserving of a high quality service. In addition, staff collaboration is likely to be well developed. It is possible to be fairly confident about these claims, as there is now a wealth of research evidence to support the notion that some school cultures are more effective than others.

Some thoughts on culture

As school culture or ethos seems to be so important it is worth being clear about its meaning. *Culture* in its broadest sense can be defined as the 'way of life' of an entire society. This includes the codes of manners, dress, language, rituals, norms and beliefs held by people in the society in question. Within societies there are also *sub-cultures*: a system of beliefs, values and norms shared by an appreciable minority of people within a particular culture.

Just as societies can be analysed and explained in terms of cultures and sub-cultures so can organisations, where culture can be seen as 'an amalgam of the values, norms and beliefs that characterise the way in which a group of people behave within a specific organisational setting' (Ainscow 1994 p. 9). Middle managers in all walks of life, including education, operate in the context of wider organisational cultures, which influence and restrain their actions, encouraging some forms of behaviour and making others more difficult. Just as in wider society, organisations can contain sub-cultural groups, operating in ways that are at odds with the dominant culture. It is important for team leaders in primary schools to be aware of this basic organisational sociology, as many of the challenges they face and frustrations they feel will be able to be explained through a consideration of organisational cultures and sub-cultures.

Considerable research has been undertaken and much has now been written about school cultures but it is important to bear two things in mind as the evidence is considered:

- First, schools exist to prepare pupils for adult life. Most teachers would accept that they have a duty to do the best they can for each child both in terms of academic achievement and in helping them to develop an outlook that will enable them to become responsible and active citizens in a democratic country. The culture of a school has a direct bearing on both of these aims and that is why getting the culture right is so important. 'The challenge is to move schools to develop responsive cultures for the moral purpose of more effectively working with students and parents to enhance the level of student learning' (Davies and West-Burnham 1997).
- Second, there is now much evidence from OFSTED reports and other sources to show that even in schools where the dominant culture leaves much to be desired, sub-cultures and even individual teachers can thrive, working in ways that are more effective and result in higher achievement levels for their pupils.

Team leaders who find themselves in badly managed schools can take heart from this. While it is difficult to swim against the tide real progress is possible and effective team leaders can become real *change agents* in a school. With regular inspections now a feature of the education system, all schools are rising to the challenge of developing cultures which match those of the most successful schools, and outdated and ineffective school cultures, like the dinosaurs, will simply not survive this process of evolution.

Organisational cultures

Handy and Aitken (1986) and Fullan and Hargreaves (1992) have identified a number of cultures relating to schools as organisations. Aspects of these cultures can still be found in many schools and they provide a useful starting point for middle managers wanting to reflect on the functioning of the organisation in which they work. When considering these cultures do bear in mind that, as with leadership styles, the pure form may not exist, as schools will reflect these cultures in varying degrees. However, organisations are likely to display distinct traits from one or more of these cultures and there is likely to be a dominant culture or ethos, best summed up as 'the way we do things around here'.

The role culture

Here the organisation is traditional and hierarchical. There are clear job descriptions and role boundaries, formalised communication and procedures and an emphasis on individuals keeping to their area of expertise. Schools that fit this model are usually well managed but not necessarily led by people with vision. They are efficient and well suited to a stable world, but schools of this type are not well equipped for coping with the rapid changes that are now a permanent feature of education.

The club culture

Here the organisation has a head teacher who cultivates the support of like-minded colleagues. Circles of intimates develop and can have greater influence than formal post holders who fall outside the 'club'. The head in such schools often uses power in an arbitrary way, rather than following agreed procedures; decisions are often made informally through discussions with the 'in-crowd' and few things are written down. Such organisations can be exciting places to work for people who have the head's patronage but other colleagues can feel marginalised and unimportant. The nepotism that exists in these schools is certainly unfair and works against principles of equal opportunities, and the reliance placed on the head teacher is very unhealthy.

The task culture

Warmth, friendliness and cooperation with little evidence of hierarchy are features of the task culture. People work as teams and groups can be changed or disbanded as the task changes. Such cultures aid problem solving and enable all individuals to contribute to moving the organisation forward. There is open questioning of past procedures and a commitment to improving the services provided. Young, energetic and self-confident people thrive in such communities. The task culture is liked neither by people who cling to job titles for security nor by people who feel threatened by 'young blood'.

The person culture

In organisations where a person culture exists professional autonomy is seen as important. The organisation allows individuals to display their talents and managers interfere as little as possible, leaving the 'experts' to get on with the job. Professionals are persuaded, influenced, cajoled and bargained with but not commanded or instructed. Teachers working in schools thirty years ago had autonomy and procedures and monitoring which are now commonplace would have been anathema. While the person culture in its pure form is now rare there are still echoes of it which, in part, explains why some managers are still reluctant to challenge the behaviour of some colleagues, even when their performance is of an unacceptable level.

The individualistic culture

Here people work in isolation. There is little collaboration and sharing of ideas and people rarely receive feedback on performance. People avoid innovation and risk taking and new ideas are not embraced. Individuals do not seek or welcome help and there is little incentive to improve performance, even though individuals may have high expectations of themselves. When meetings do take place few people contribute and even interaction at a social level is rare. There is a danger that individualised cultures can develop in large primary schools where the only meetings which take place involve all staff and where the agenda is dominated by administrative matters.

The balkanised culture

In balkanised schools teachers develop loyalty to separate groups and there is competition between groups. Year groups or Key Stage teams behave like nation states and distinct sub-cultures exist which make working with a common ethos difficult. There is a lack of communication between groups and a tendency to assume negative stereotypes about members of other groups. Conflict over use of space (e.g. hall, library, outside play areas) and resources (e.g. TV, PE equipment, the laminator) is common. In balkanised schools making a success of whole-school initiatives is very difficult.

The collaborative culture

In schools where a collaborative culture exists there is a clear and shared vision about the values and purposes of the school and this vision is regularly reviewed and examined. Teachers' voices are strong, disagreements are visible and teachers are both empowered and accountable. Team teaching and joint planning are common, teachers are willing to be learners and there is a commitment to ongoing professional development. Teams work effectively and there is a high level of trust and openness. Hierarchies are not so obvious and banter, jokes and celebrations reflect mutual understanding and respect.

As you consider these cultures it is worth thinking about the following questions:
- Which culture do you associate with the organisation you work in?
- Can more than one culture be present in the same organisation?
- In which culture would change occur most easily?
- What effect would each of these cultures have on students?
- Which school culture would generate the most positive school ethos?
- How can middle managers help to change the school culture?

Clearly, schools which are successful in today's educational world are those which can respond to change effectively. The task culture and the club culture would seem most appropriate for this. However, as we have seen, the club culture is unlikely to get the best out of *all* colleagues. Although the era of the person culture as described above has now passed, many successful heads try to provide autonomy for their staff, set in the context of clear goals and a strategic vision, as a way of creating a dynamic culture. The collaborative culture best fits the evidence emerging about successful schools and it is the approach currently being promoted in much literature on school effectiveness and through management training.

At the heart of the collaborative culture is the idea that schools can develop and improve only through the creative involvement of all those who work in them. The unfortunate divide which has emerged in some schools between 'managers' and 'teachers' needs to be broken down so that all can contribute their skills to achieving an agreed vision. This *empowerment* helps to generate commitment and means that all teachers, regardless of their job title, can contribute their skills and enthusiasm to moving a school forward.

> An important aspect of the character of effective schools is that management is not the unique task of those at the apex of a hierarchy but a shared responsibility of all who are involved in the school. A culture which proclaims that heads (and deputies) manage but teachers teach is not conducive to effective development. (Hargreaves and Hopkins 1991)

Linking this to management styles considered in Chapter 2, it is clear that a Whiteheadian outlook is required if a collaborative culture is to be achieved. Staff must be valued, recognised as professionals and assumed to want to do their best for the children they teach. This does not, of course, mean colleagues are simply left to their own devices. As we saw in Chapter 1, schools serious about quality have in place mechanisms for monitoring staff performance and pupil achievement. Schools in which a positive ethos is instantly recognisable are likely to have in place sensible structures, procedures and monitoring, balanced with a good deal of individual autonomy for both staff and students.

School culture and effectiveness

In 1993 a report was produced for the Department for Education on effective school management. A total of fifty seven schools (primary, secondary and special) were involved in the survey and the staff in those schools recognised the following as contributing to effective management practice which helped to generate a positive school ethos:

- Students play an active part in the life of the school and there are high expectations of them in terms of behaviour and achievement.
- Complacency among staff is actively discouraged in favour of a questioning, critical attitude.
- There is an open atmosphere; staff respect one another and talk freely about professional matters.
- Staff are involved in developing the school's aims and policies.
- All staff have a clear understanding of the school's vision.
- The head is accessible to staff and has a consultative 'listening' style.
- The head praises staff and celebrates their achievements.
- The SMT delegate tasks to develop and empower staff but also monitor performance.
- Working parties operate to reach decisions and write policies.
- Struggling staff are supported.
- Staff feel valued and their views are taken seriously.
- Professional development for all staff is encouraged.
- Many decisions are made collaboratively.

This is not the complete list, but the points above are useful in guiding us to a conclusion regarding effective school cultures. A good summary is provided by Ainscow (1994) who suggests, 'the type of school cultures most supportive of school improvement efforts are those that are collaborative, have high expectations for both students and staff, exhibit a consensus of values, and support an orderly and secure environment'. Many of these features are to be found in schools aiming for a collaborative model of organisation. While the existence of these features will not be a guarantee that *all* staff in schools displaying them will be motivated, involved and productive, it is more likely that a *critical mass* of the staff will be.

Further evidence of effective school cultures was provided by Sammons *et al.* (1995). They were commissioned by OFSTED to undertake a review of international school effectiveness literature, particularly from the United Kingdom, North America and the Netherlands. They were asked to assess whether or not, despite very different approaches to education in different countries, successful schools had common distinctive features. They came up with eleven key characteristics found in effective schools in all the countries studied:

- Professional leadership which encourages participation.
- Shared vision and goals generated by collegiality and collaboration.
- An orderly learning environment.
- A focus on achievement.
- Purposeful teaching.
- High expectations.
- Positive reinforcement.
- Effective monitoring of progress.
- Active involvement of pupils.
- Parental involvement.
- A strong emphasis on staff development.

Once again, the collaborative culture is in evidence, suggesting that this approach is the most likely to generate success in primary schools. In management literature the collaborative culture is associated with collegial models of management.

Collegiality

Collegial models assume that organisations determine policy and make decisions through a process of discussion leading to consensus. Power is shared among some or all members of the organisation who are thought to have a mutual understanding about the objectives of the institution.   (Bush 1994)

Middle managers working in schools which have developed such an approach have the advantage that most colleagues in their teams are likely to be receptive to team work, sharing ideas and working towards agreed goals. This does not, however, mean that *all* colleagues will be. Middle managers not working in schools with a collaborative/ collegiate culture may find it more difficult to involve their teams in new ways of working, but changing 'the way we do things around here' is possible. How managers can begin to support colleagues in changing their practice is a theme covered in Chapter 4.

Case studies

Below can be found 'thumb nail' descriptions of two schools. Read each one and then reflect on the questions that follow.

Study 1

Sandgate Primary is a good school. Parents say so to one another. It achieves good results at the end of Key Stage 1 and 2. The children all wear uniform and discipline is firm. 'Miss Reynolds (the head teacher) runs a tight ship' is a remark often made by the Chair of Governors. The staff know exactly where they stand. They have clear job descriptions which were drawn up by the Head and as long as they work hard at maintaining good discipline and end of Key Stage 1 and 2 results, they will continue to hold the respect of Miss Reynolds, the governors and the parents.

Union concern over bureaucracy and the unnecessary pressure it places on teaching staff is not seen as an issue. The school's policies have been in place for many years and as they appear to work for the most part, there is no obvious need to change them. Staff meetings are short and to the point and are used to deal largely with administrative matters.

National strategies have been introduced and put into operation exactly in the form outlined in DfEE documentation. No debate on these matters is considered important or necessary. The curriculum emphasis has always been on teaching the basics with the other subjects being given much less time, apart from drama. Miss Reynolds personally organises two drama concerts each year, which the parents of the children involved consider, are 'equal to anything that the West End can produce'.

Parents are kept informed of the happenings in school by a succinct clear termly newsletter, which contains the dates and a line of information on each event. Information on the progress of each child is given to parents at each of the three consultation evenings (one per term). The school achieves an average of 98 per cent attendance at these meetings during the year.

Study 2

Mountside Primary is a good school, or at least many parents think so. It achieves good results at the end of Key Stage 1 and 2. The children are actively encouraged to wear school uniform and the behaviour management policy requires children to take responsibility for their own actions, but sanctions are rigorously applied to those pupils who choose to break the agreed school rules. However, the Canteen Supervisor thinks the Head, Mrs Khan, should do more about discipline in school. The staff have clear job descriptions which they have written and agreed with the Head. They have copies of all the policy documents which have been drawn up and agreed, sometimes as a result of prolonged staff discussion. Staff are expected to apply the agreed policies but some do it better than others and parents and governors are aware of this. Union concern over bureaucracy means some meetings which Mrs Khan feels need to take place do not occur. She has deep concerns about national strategies being implemented without discussion and debate taking place.

The curriculum emphasis in the school is very much on providing the children with a broad and balanced curriculum. There is an emphasis on the basics but the staff have agreed on the amount of time which each of the other subjects in the primary curriculum should receive. Pupils are provided with the opportunity to be involved in a wide range of extra curricular activities. Elections in connection with the School Council take place each year for pupils in Years 5 and 6.

Half termly chatty newsletters keep parents informed of the numerous events occurring in school. Although the school holds formal consultation evenings, parents can make appointments to see class teachers at any time. A few parents take advantage of this facility. Attendance at parent consultation evenings average 95 per cent at the first two consultation evenings but only 20 per cent at the end of the year. The July evening is held to allow parents the opportunity to discuss their child's end of year written report with the teacher.

Reflection

- What type of organisational culture can be applied to (i) Sandgate Primary (ii) Mountside Primary?
- As a middle manager what do you consider to be the strengths and weaknesses of each school? In which school would you prefer to be employed? Why?
- Consider why working for a head teacher who believed in the collaborative culture might be better for a middle manager than working for a head who favoured some other culture.
- If you were a parent in the catchment area, which of these two schools do you think you would prefer your child/ren to attend? Why?
- If it is true that, basically, schools are helping to prepare their pupils for the world of work and life in general, which school

(Sandgate or Mountside) do you consider is doing the better job? Why?

Summary

Institutions of all kinds display different cultures or 'ways of doing things' and schools are no exception. In recent years, a range of school cultures has been identified by researchers and there is now a considerable body of evidence indicating that primary schools which adopt a collegiate approach to management are the most effective. This style is now being encouraged in management literature as a means of improving school effectiveness and there are cases on record of this approach being employed to assist in turning round failing schools.

A collegiate approach is likely to generate a collaborative ethos, characterised by a clear vision, staff involvement in decision making and a culture of critical reflection, learning from peers and professional development. Teachers working in a collaborative culture are likely to have considerable autonomy, flexibility and responsibility, within a framework of monitoring and evaluation of their performance. There is also likely to be much discussion about how to improve teaching and learning and it is possible that pupils themselves could be involved in this.

To be effective in such cultures middle managers need to be good team players, supportive, self-critical, reflective and not frightened by the prospect of empowering colleagues in their teams. They will not be concerned by status, hierarchy and the kind of power that comes from rigid job descriptions. They will be good at delegating and will take pride in allowing others in their team to flower and grow. Middle managers not working in schools characterised by collaborative features can still achieve a great deal of collegiality within their own teams. However, while some staff not used to working collegially will rise to the challenge, others may be reluctant and fearful and will need careful nurturing away from the state of dependency they have been allowed (or forced) to exist in.

CHAPTER FOUR

Getting the Best Out of People

Introduction

During the 1970s students undergoing teacher-training devoted a lot of time to discussing what was the best approach to educating young people. One school of thought was that young people should be seen as empty pots, waiting to be filled with knowledge which we, the teachers, defined as valuable. Our level of education and experience, so the argument went, provided us with the necessary authority to decide what was best for the pupils in our care. This was challenged by those who saw children as being more like delicate plants which, when provided with the right environment, would develop naturally to reveal their full beauty. Too much shaping and pruning, it was argued, would hinder development. What was needed was stimulation not control.

These debates and discussions were over-simplified and polarised into what became seen in the media as a choice between 'traditional' and 'progressive' teaching methods and what teachers in some schools saw as a choice between 'passive' and 'active' learning. The legislative changes of the last twenty years, especially the introduction of the National Curriculum and school inspection, have removed the likelihood of teachers being able to maintain either of the extreme and simplified positions outlined above. Good practice in the classroom involves combining both approaches. What successful primary teachers are able to do is differentiate between classes, and individuals within classes, in terms of the balance of passivity and activity required for effective learning to occur.

There are very real similarities between successful teaching, which enables children to develop, and effective management, which enables members of a team to improve their skills and potential. While team leaders in school are usually well aware of the need to differentiate when planning lessons in order to help all pupils to progress, they do not always apply the same logic to the nurturing of people in their teams. Indeed, there are still some 'authoritarian' managers who treat junior colleagues rather like empty pots and some laissez-faire managers who imagine that people in their teams will magically develop if they are simply left alone to do so.

Middle managers should see helping colleagues to develop professionally as a duty. Effective teachers assess children in order to plan their learning programmes, and good managers think carefully about the needs of their team members in order to help them develop their skills and abilities. Clearly, a newly qualified teacher entering a primary school will have quite different needs from a very experienced teacher who has signalled a desire to retire early. It is important for middle managers not just to realise this but to act upon it. Before they can do this, however, team leaders must develop an understanding of what motivates people and must strive to develop good practice in their handling of colleagues, just as teachers must develop good classroom organisation and discipline before they can turn their attention to differentiation.

What motivates people?

Psychologists and sociologists have produced many theories that attempt to explain what motivates people in work. Over the years various companies have experimented with altering the working environment, providing financial rewards for increases in productivity and using a range of sticks and carrots in order to get the best out of their employees. In education, the production of performance tables based on national tests and exam results has made target setting for schools possible and it seems likely that some kind of performance related pay will be introduced into education in the future. At the time of writing this book thousands of teachers had just applied to cross the *performance threshold* and head teachers were busy drafting a performance framework for their schools. It is possible that regular appraisal of teachers and target setting will improve results in areas that are easily measured. However, this approach does not always generate a sense of loyalty to a school and can, in fact, be counter productive if teachers cease to give time to areas of school life which are not so easily measured. Middle managers need to make use of appraisal and targets (see Chapter 10) but there is much else that can be done to motivate colleagues.

In the commercial world companies have come to appreciate the importance of developing loyalty in their workers. Through initiatives such as 'Investors in People' they have attempted to organise themselves in ways which show that their human resources are valued. Increasingly, companies have a *mission statement* and employees are encouraged to share the company's *vision* and help the organisation move towards achieving its goals. Schools, also, are beginning to use these techniques as a way of helping to create a clear and shared sense of purpose. It is obvious that teachers are the most important resource in schools and their commitment is vital to the success of any improvement initiatives.

> Of all the resources at the disposal of an organisation it is only people who can grow and develop and be motivated to achieve certain desired ends. The attaining of targets is in their hands and it is the way people are managed . . . which is at the heart of human resource management . . . and optimum management.
>
> (Riches and Morgan 1989 p. 1)

It is essential, therefore, actively to engage teachers in the shaping of the school and to ensure that they feel valued and in possession of high levels of skill. As indicated in Chapter 2 and Chapter 3 democratic leadership styles and collaborative school cultures are more likely to generate success and commitment from most teachers than other approaches. This can partly be explained by the ideas of Abraham Maslow.

Maslow produced a theory of motivation that sought to go beyond financial and environmental considerations when explaining employee behaviour. This theory, conceived in the 1950s, still has much to commend it and certainly seems to explain why so many teachers work as hard as they do with seemingly little financial reward. According to Maslow there are various needs that humans have to satisfy and these should be seen as a hierarchy. More basic or low-level needs, he argued, must be satisfied before a higher need becomes important (see Figure 4.1). The lowest order needs are physiological ones: hunger, thirst and warmth. In most cases, people at work have already satisfied these needs through having money to pay for them. Regarding safety needs, Maslow argues that, in today's society, these only act as motivators at times of crises that threaten safety or life, such as fire, natural catastrophes, crime waves and other emergency situations. Social needs, however, do act as motivators in the workplace as most people need to feel they *belong*. Most people don't

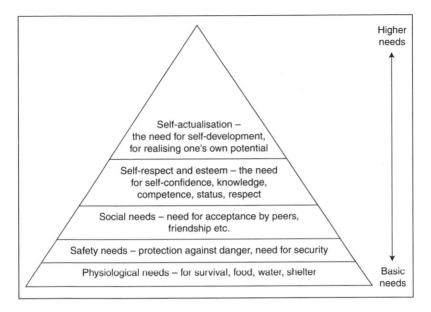

Figure 4.1 Maslow's hierarchy of needs

just go to work to put in the hours so that they can earn enough money to enjoy the time they are not at work. If the work satisfies social needs, the next stage in the hierarchy is that of esteem needs. To have self-esteem you need to feel a sense of achievement in what you do and to gain the respect of those you work with; from self-esteem stem feelings of self-confidence and self-worth. According to Maslow *self-actualisation* is the most developed level, and not all humans will manage to reach it. Self-actualisation, the need for self-development and realising one's potential, is certainly what drives many teachers. It is not possible to generalise, of course, but many teachers are not overly materialistic and often seem more motivated by a genuine desire to achieve their full potential and that of their pupils than by financial rewards.

Motivating others through good practice

Maslow's hierarchy shows us that people are motivated by a range of needs and may be motivated in different ways at different stages of their life. However, the importance Maslow places on higher level needs provides valuable insights into people's motivation and gives us a useful starting point for some general rules on good practice for managers. If Maslow's contention that people are driven by the desire for acceptance by peers, self-respect, and self-actualisation is correct then managers would be wise to reflect on their behaviour towards colleagues in terms of how it affects their feelings of acceptance, their self-respect and their opportunity for self-actualisation. Listening to teachers complaining about the way they have been treated by managers adds weight to Maslow's theory and also to the importance of creating collaborative school cultures (discussed in Chapter 3).

The following statements apply to most, though not all, teachers:

- Teachers like to be consulted about what they have to do – just being told what to do does not generate feelings of *ownership* for a particular policy.
- Teachers appreciate managers who are willing to listen – feeling that their views are of no significance is demotivating.
- Teachers appreciate being seen as valuable individuals with specialist skills – being seen as a mere cog in the machine, easily replaced by other cogs, does not build self-esteem.
- Teachers respond to sensitive managers – heavy-handed use of authority is often counter productive.
- Teachers perform better when they enjoy their work and feel relaxed – managers who can spread good cheer and empower teachers will be helping to motivate them.
- Teachers whose successes are recognised become more successful and more motivated – praise for teachers is as important as praise for their pupils.

From these statements it is not difficult to arrive at some general though important pointers on good practice for middle managers.

1. Spend time getting to know the people in your team and then support them

When you become a middle manager it is worth spending time getting to know the people for whom you have a management responsibility. Your knowledge of the people in your team will help you to manage situations more easily, for example by being able to anticipate people's likely reactions to new ideas. As you get to know people you will become concerned for their welfare and as this begins to show it is likely to bring you greater loyalty than managers who stand aloof. Showing that you are interested in colleagues as people and as professionals will encourage the members of your team to offer you the support that you will need to do your job effectively.

Getting to know colleagues is sure to make you want to help them to do their best and this will make you a better manager. The Key Stage Coordinator who tries to support team members who are looking under the weather, by taking their break duty, for example, will not only help to prevent them 'going under' (thus saving work) but will also earn goodwill which is likely to be repaid many times over. This makes management sense, but the desire to support comes also from a genuine wish to help colleagues you have taken the time to get to know.

2. *Communicate clearly with your team and don't be frightened by debate*

It is important that people in your team do not feel they are being kept in the dark about important new developments. Talk to colleagues about any plans or schemes and ask for their ideas. Remember that any initiatives you think up are unlikely to succeed without the support of a *critical mass* of team members. Always explain things clearly. People are more likely to cooperate if they know what they are supposed to be doing. If you are putting in place a policy generated externally to your team, for example responding to new legislation, or initiated by the head teacher, involve your colleagues as much as possible in deciding *how* the scheme will operate in your area.

A sense of ownership is really important if a new initiative is to succeed. Your team should not just be briefed about it but should have the chance to talk it through in a free and open exchange of views. This can act as a real safety valve, allowing people to share their worries and concerns. When there is no dialogue, people will be more likely to begin muttering in small groups and in these circumstances dissatisfaction can soon take hold.

3. *Make decisions!*

While it is important to consult people in your team and to keep them informed about important developments it is not necessary to involve all team members in every decision that has to be made. One of your responsibilities as a manager is to shield colleagues from trivia and minutiae so that they are free to devote their energies to the children in their classrooms. Colleagues would, quite rightly, be annoyed if you allocated teaching groups without consultation but there is nothing to be gained in consulting your team about whether or not to order another box of white-board markers!

Those decisions that require time, thought and consultation will still need resolution and expecting colleagues to attend many long meetings is unrealistic. Taking the time to make a good decision is one thing – being indecisive is quite another, and is fatal if you want to be an effective manager. Involving people in making important decisions is good and getting people *on side* will increase the likelihood of success. However, not all decisions can be democratic and it is not always possible to get everyone in your team to be enthusiastic about every initiative. Finally, if you realise that a decision you made was wrong don't be afraid to admit it. Managers who are open about their mistakes (unless mistakes are made all the time) earn more respect than those who insist on pushing ahead with flawed plans.

4. *Display self-control and be positive*

Good managers calmly find ways to solve problems and they do not make mountains out of molehills. Respect is more likely to be gained by being calm when things go wrong than by creating anxiety in others by exaggerating the importance of small mistakes they have made. You will soon lose the respect of colleagues if you constantly challenge them over minor matters and this will make tackling major issues more difficult. There is nothing constructive in interrogating members of your team about a missing pencil sharpener! However, if stock control is an issue of concern then it can be put on the agenda for a team meeting so that all can have their say. Some managers are so obsessed with insignificant day-to-day matters that they never properly address the really important issues. Indeed, over attention to detail can be a method employed, perhaps unconsciously, to avoid having to face more difficult decisions and can sometimes be a sign that the manager in question is suffering serious stress. Remember, as a manager you will never reach the hilltop if you allow yourself to get bogged down in the mud in the valley.

5. *Lead by example*

You cannot expect other people to do what you are not able or prepared to do yourself. As a team leader you should set a high standard in the amount and the quality of the work you do and in your general attitude to your pupils. You cannot grumble about your workload and show cynicism for whole-school initiatives and then expect people in your team enthusiastically to embrace new ideas you have. You cannot allocate all the highly motivated children to your class and then complain to colleagues about the behaviour or results of their groups. In short, you have to lead from the front.

Some managers find it difficult to admit their own weaknesses. It is vital that you share your classroom failures as well as your successes with your team if you expect them to be open with you about their weaknesses. Creating a genuinely collaborative team ethos requires openness and critical self-reflection from everyone; this is much more likely to be achieved if the team leader makes it clear that he or she understands that nobody can be excellent at everything. This is not an excuse for poor performance, but the foundation stone of a team culture that enables all members to improve by learning from, and supporting, one another.

6. Be considerate and fair

The maxim 'treat other people as you would wish to be treated yourself' is an important one for middle managers. This means more than simply being pleasant and friendly towards others; it means thinking about the impact your actions will have on their self-esteem and motivation. It also means not forgetting that members of your team may have responsibilities in other areas of school and are entitled to a family life. You cannot expect people to drop what they are doing to fit into your plans just because you are the team leader. Consult your colleagues before you arrange a trip or 'team' activity so that you can choose a time and date which suits the majority. If you are fair with your team you will get more out of them and when there is a genuine crisis which requires them to change their plans at short notice, they are more likely to try and help you out.

One of the ways in which fairness becomes transparent is the willingness to accept to take a different year group or class or change classrooms. It is important that the criteria for year group, class, and room allocation is clear to everyone. A member of staff historically being allocated a particular room is not of itself a good reason for continuing the practice. It is a manager's duty to ensure that younger colleagues are nurtured, developed and treated fairly.

7. Listen to people

The ability to listen carefully and, when necessary, sympathetically is an important skill for any team leader. Middle managers should be willing to listen properly to the concerns of individuals in their teams and need to be accessible. This does not mean dropping everything at the precise moment someone mentions something to you; if necessary arrange another time that suits you both. It is important to remember when arranging such meetings that things usually take longer to discuss than you (or they) estimate they will. Being willing to give up time to help people is an important aspect of management responsibility and should not be regarded as a burden, even though it will take you away from other aspects of your role. You should regard time spent listening as a good investment as it really can help you to nip problems in the bud, and by supporting colleagues through difficult times you are helping to nurture the collaborative and supportive culture which will allow your team to flourish.

Middle managers should also be skilled in assessing the mood of a meeting, by listening carefully to what is being said. The democratic leader should not expect always to have the last word. When people are talking they deserve your full attention and when they have finished their contribution it is useful to sum up their ideas to make sure you have grasped fully what they have said. When new ideas are being proposed people's initial response can often be to focus on the negatives. This is understandable, as people are generally cautious when it comes to change, not least because extra work is likely to be involved. Be patient and allow people their say. It is amazing how soon a real debate will begin and, if the new idea is a good one, how quickly the proposals will be embraced. Trying to force your ideas on people without debate is counter productive and undermines collaboration and trust.

8. *Spread good cheer!*

The ability to spread good cheer should be an essential quality listed on selection criteria sheets sent to prospective candidates for management posts in the school! The importance of this should never be underestimated. In far too many staff rooms you will find disgruntled middle managers being negative and cynical. No doubt individual cynics will have their personal reasons for their lack of enthusiasm, but they are being unprofessional and failing in their duties as managers through their actions. Keeping up staff morale is a central role of middle managers and it can be achieved in quite small, but very significant, ways.

Always give credit where it is due and always give praise and thanks when it is deserved. Often this will be done in a one-to-one situation but praising individuals in the presence of others (at a staff meeting or a staff briefing) should occur when colleagues have special achievements worthy of sharing. Take pride in announcing what people in your team have achieved and never see their successes as a threat to your status. Managers should be judged, at least in part, by what they have allowed and encouraged those in their teams to achieve. It is especially important to praise newly qualified teachers in the presence of a third party as you are trying to build their confidence and socialise them into the supportive culture of your team.

Praise, thanks and attention provide what are called *positive strokes* and these help to build up morale and confidence. We all want to be appreciated and valued but, sadly, it often feels like the media and government have little that is positive to say about teachers. This can undermine morale and self-confidence and makes it all the more difficult to motivate staff. It is true that success breeds success and it is also true that negative talk can create failure or at least sap enthusiasm. By spreading good cheer and publicising achievement middle managers help to keep up the morale of their teams and help individuals to feel valued and appreciated.

With the above foundation stones of good practice in place it will be easier to handle difficult issues which you encounter (such as the poor performance of a colleague) and to consider the individual development needs of members of your team.

Situational leadership

In Chapter 2 it was suggested that a democratic approach to management in education was desirable and in Chapter 3 empowerment and autonomy for colleagues was encouraged. However, not *all* teachers respond to the good practice of democratic management and not *all* teachers are capable of acting autonomously. This is where situational leadership becomes important as a way of dealing with colleagues with different levels of professional competence.

Schools that have embraced the 'Investors in People' approach regard all staff as internal clients and, therefore, meeting their development needs is a natural function of the organisation. In all schools helping teachers and support staff to develop and improve their skills is obviously central to improving the achievement of pupils. While being fair and consistent with all members of your team it is important to remember that 'there is nothing so unequal as the equal treatment of unequals' (Blanchard 1994). Teachers know this to be true in meeting the needs of the pupils they teach; it is also true for managers addressing the professional development needs of people in their teams.

Effective managers, therefore, need to be flexible in the management styles they use (even if their ideal style is democratic) depending on the individuals they are dealing with. The choice of style used will depend on an assessment of the needs of the individual concerned. This assessment may be formal through, say, appraisal (see Chapter 11) but is more likely to be instinctive, based on day-to-day observation and discussion with colleagues. A collaborative culture makes it much easier for a manager to slip naturally between the situational leadership styles outlined in Table 4.1.

All of these styles have their uses for middle managers and experienced team leaders move so easily between them that individuals on the receiving end are often unaware of different approaches being used with different team members. If they are aware they are rarely disgruntled by it, as skilful managers are operating within a culture of trust and support which they have created. Indeed, in an effective team it will not just be the team leader who is using these styles but all colleagues, as they support one another.

A consideration of these four styles reveals a balance between directive behaviour and supportive behaviour. Directive behaviour involves telling people what to do, how to do it, when to do it, and then monitoring performance. Supportive behaviour involves listening to people, providing support and encouragement, and facilitating involvement in decision making. Different circumstances and different individuals require different combinations of directive and supportive behaviour and middle managers will need to use careful judgements when considering the best approach to adopt. In general though the styles can be applied to team members as shown in Table 4.2.

Typically, a directing style would be used when inducting new teachers into certain team procedures. A coaching style might be used

Directing	Coaching	Supporting	Delegating
The leader provides very clear and specific direction and closely monitors results achieved	The leader directs and supervises but also explains decisions, encourages suggestions and supports progress	The leader facilitates and supports team members in decision making and accomplishing tasks	The leader delegates responsibility for decision making and task completion to team members

Table 4.1 Situational leadership styles

Style	Characteristics of team member
Directing	Low level of competence but high level of commitment
Coaching	Basic level of competence but low level of commitment
Supporting	High level of competence but variable level of commitment
Delegating	High level of competence and high level of commitment

Table 4.2 Situational style and characteristics of team member

with colleagues who have been identified as under-performing in some aspect of their work. A supporting style is the style that is likely to be used most often and is in harmony with a democratic approach to management. Delegation can be used with experienced and committed colleagues and is especially useful for providing ambitious and competent teachers with experiences that might help them gain promotion to management posts. However, it is important to remember that people's level of competence and commitment can vary with different aspects of their jobs. It is possible, for example, to find very competent and committed teachers who nevertheless lack well developed IT skills and may need coaching or even directing in this area. Equally, newly qualified teachers may bring high levels of IT skills into a team, even though they need directing in school and team procedures.

Team leaders (and class teachers) are likely to find themselves managing people other than teachers. Student teachers, non-teaching assistants, special needs support assistants, nursery nurses and parent helpers all have to be 'managed'. While the same situational leadership styles can be applied to these members of your team, it is important to remember that people who have not been through teacher training may require much more directing and coaching. Also, there are, quite rightly, clear limits to the exact roles being performed by each of these groups. This doesn't alter the fact that effective use and development of non-teaching staff can make a major impact on class management and pupil progress. Middle managers must not be reluctant to direct non-teaching colleagues; they are usually keen to do the best they can for the pupils they support and welcome clear guidance and direction, especially when they are new to their role. All colleagues and helpers involved in a school deserve to be treated with respect and made to feel valued, and time spent with non-teaching team members should be regarded as an investment that will pay dividends in the future.

Middle managers who have to deal with members of their teams who are encountering difficulties usually find this the most stressful and difficult aspect of their work. Helping colleagues to improve their performance is certainly a management challenge. However, struggling colleagues cannot be ignored and middle managers who fail to address their development needs let down not just the struggling colleague but the children in their care. The needs of the vast majority of teachers can be met by appropriate support from their team leader. But, in situations where there are serious weaknesses, it is vital to involve senior managers in deciding on the best way to handle such colleagues (see Chapter 11).

Some thoughts on coaching

Managers in school should also be successful teachers. They have well-developed skills and competencies worth sharing with less experienced colleagues and teachers undergoing initial training. Good managers share their skills in the hope that members of their team can become as effective or more effective in the classroom than they are. They also facilitate opportunities for other colleagues in their teams to share good practice, with continuously improving performance being a central aim.

Coaching involves helping other persons to develop their skills and knowledge: 'passing on your experience to someone else rather as masters did to apprentices in the past. It should be a rewarding experience for both the coach and the learner; if it is not, then the coaching is not being effective' (Thomson 1998).

Coaching is time consuming and it requires paying attention to:
• the learner's precise needs;
• the learner's preferred learning style; and
• developing the learning skills of the learner.

Teachers generally make good coaches as they are used to using coaching skills with the children they teach. Middle managers need not do all the coaching themselves. It is good experience for other colleagues to undertake coaching and helps to develop their communication skills and self-confidence. As with teaching and management there is no single coaching style for all situations. A careful analysis of a range of factors will determine the style adopted. A protective, kindly and reassuring approach might be used with a teacher who lacks confidence whereas a tougher and more demanding style might be employed on a capable but lazy colleague. Always try and think through what the consequences of choosing a particular style will be. Sometimes, several people have similar needs and can be coached together. Subject Coordinators and Key Stage Coordinators, in particular, can use their meetings as an opportunity to coach the rest of the team.

Case studies

The following comments, made to Peter Fleming by different teachers over the years, illustrate just how motivational Maslow's notion of 'higher needs' can be.

Study 1

'I am absolutely determined to do a brilliant job with this class. The head teacher has trusted me with Year 6, even though I've not taught at the top end of the school before. I'm determined that we'll get the best Key Stage 2 results ever!' (Primary teacher in her third year of teaching.)

Study 2

'I know it's a lot of money, but I'm doing this for myself. If school can't pay the fees I will pay them. I've told myself for years that once my children are old enough I'll study for a Masters and that's what I'm determined to do.' (Middle aged applicant for M.Ed degree.)

Study 3

'I am more interested in gaining this post for the challenge than the money. A few hundred pounds won't make much difference to my life-style; I just feel ready for a change, a new challenge, a different role. I'm very happy at this school and I know I'm respected but I feel as if I've not yet achieved my full potential – and I don't want to regret that later in life.' (Colleague discussing applying for a deputy head post in a new primary school.)

Study 4

'I felt really deflated, as if he didn't trust me. I know I'm capable of producing a brilliant magazine and the kids are so keen. He kept

53

saying I needed more experience before starting something so major and he kept going on about the time and effort needed. Surely I'm the best judge of how much time I can give and I really wanted to prove I could handle this.' (Teacher with two years' experience, after speaking to her Key Stage Coordinator about taking on responsibility for the school magazine.)

Reflection

There is much to be learnt from these examples. You have probably met many colleagues who work very hard indeed in response to being given responsibilities that boost their self-confidence. Often the responsibility they had been given was unpaid, but the effect it had on their self-esteem was tremendous. Making people feel skilled, trusted and valued are strong motivators indeed. Just think of the hours many teachers devote to making a success of summer fayres and other such activities they are given responsibility for, usually for no financial reward whatsoever.

Market research indicates that about half the teachers undertaking part-time study towards a higher degree pay their own fees. Many of them feel that gaining such a qualification will improve their chances of promotion but for others the desire for self-actualisation is what drives them. Likewise, many teachers who take on promoted posts do so as much for self-development as for the small financial reward that is so often involved. Many people enter teaching from a genuine desire, a calling, to work with young people. These teachers represent a significant proportion of the profession and, when managed effectively, show great motivation.

Middle managers must help members of their team to develop. It is demotivating and deskilling (as in Case study 4) to reject the suggestions of team members without discussion and to undermine their hopes and plans. If their desires are unreasonable or genuinely incompatible with the vision of the school or the needs of your area then careful handling is required so that they can be let down gently. Likewise, if you have good reason to think a team member is being over ambitious then think of ways in which they can be supported or their plans can be modified, rather than simply rejecting them. Always try and support team members in what they want to do. Take pride in their achievements and be grateful that they are so highly motivated. Dealing with disillusioned and disgruntled colleagues is far more challenging than supporting and empowering the enthusiastic.

Summary

The Teacher Training Agency's *National Standards for Subject Leaders* includes the ability to 'deal sensitively with people, recognising individual needs and take account of these in securing a consistent team approach to raising achievement . . .' (TTA 1998) as a skill required of middle managers. This involves the flexible use of directing, coaching, supporting and delegating with team members, depending on the particular individuals and the specific issues being dealt with. Successful middle managers move between styles with sensitivity and tact, so as to help the professional development of their colleagues.

The successful application of these four styles occurs most successfully when a team ethos of support, collaboration and openness has been achieved. Such a culture is most likely to be created by managers who show a genuine interest in team members, keep people informed and seek their opinions, stay calm and remain positive, are fair, lead by example, smile and praise and publicly and sincerely celebrate the successes of team members.

Adair (1997) sums up the approach required very neatly:

The six most important words . . .
   'I admit I made a mistake.'
The five most important words . . .
   'I am proud of you.'
The four most important words . . .
   'What is your opinion?'
The three most important words . . .
   'If you please.'
The two most important words . . .
   'Thank you.'
The one most important word . . .
   'We.'
And the last, least important word . . .
   'I.'

CHAPTER FIVE

Building Your Team

Introduction

In Chapter 1 the range of primary schools in terms of size and management arrangements was discussed in order to define 'middle management' as precisely as possible. This range makes it equally difficult to generalise about teams in primary schools. Most head teachers would argue that team refers to all of the staff working in their school and would see it as their duty to develop the staff as a team. While this view is commendable, it is important to note that whereas in a small, rural primary school (operating mixed-age class groups) all staff are likely to be involved in collaboration on most issues, this would simply not be practical in a large primary school. In such schools there will be many different teams operating under the leadership of middle managers, besides the whole school team.

Some teams are permanent, for example year teams and the SMT (now Leadership Group), although membership changes as a result of staff being promoted, staff retiring or internal restructuring. Other teams are temporary, for example working groups established to write a particular policy document or plan a school production. Some teams operate very formally, for example governing bodies, whereas other teams can be quite informal, such as a group of colleagues who have taken on responsibility for organising staff social events. Some teams have limited membership, for example the SMT, whereas other teams offer open access, for instance a working party on behaviour. Membership of some teams is voluntary but membership of other teams is contractual.

Some teams are more effective than others. Indeed, it would be fair to conclude that many teams are not really teams at all but simply groups of people placed together because they teach classes containing pupils of the same age group, for example. In such groups the activities of individuals frequently limit, rather than enhance the effectiveness of the whole. There may be jealousies between members, information suppressed and cooperation withheld because members see themselves as being in competition with one another. Alternatively, there may be apathy and indifference resulting from a lack of team vision or sense of direction.

A major challenge for middle managers is to transform a group of people they have responsibility for, lumped together under some functional umbrella, into a successful team. Teams thrive best in collaborative cultures (see Chapter 3) and in situations where the team leader is committed to the development of each individual (see Chapter 4). Even then, there is still much effort and skill needed in creating and maintaining a genuine team. Where really effective teams do exist, the support which team members receive from one another, the rapport that exists and the sense of working for common goals is very powerful. A successful team becomes visible to others working in the school and it is not unusual for pupils to notice and comment upon this. It is a real achievement indeed when the atmosphere generated by a successful team is absorbed by pupils and begins to influence their behaviour.

What makes a group of people a team?

1. Vision and sense of direction

Having shared goals is the first thing that distinguishes groups from teams. This is why it is so important that the team leader has a clear sense of direction. This should be provided partly by the vision or mission of the school, with the team leader's job being to translate the vision into something meaningful at team level. A clear sense of direction will also come from the team leader being certain about what their team is uniquely contributing to the education of young people. If you are a History Coordinator then what is your vision of excellent history teaching? What can the subject uniquely contribute to the education of primary pupils? If you are a year group leader what is your vision for the year group? What can your team of teachers contribute to the education of this age group beyond the requirements of the National Curriculum? These question are fundamental, and need to be discussed and answers agreed upon by team members in order to provide both a sense of direction and an underpinning philosophy to the work of the team.

2. *The behaviour of the team leader*

It is important that leaders are able to give their teams space for development, that they can listen to the views of others and can encourage participation. Team leaders should encourage collegiality and adopt a democratic style of leadership. They must be self-critical and committed to the idea that their authority comes more from their behaviour and the example they set than from their title. Team leaders will want individuals in their team to progress and develop and will be skilful at directing, coaching, supporting and delegating, as appropriate. The team leader will be visible and accessible and will strive to build the self-esteem of all team members.

3. *The extent to which people pull together*

A team exists if members embrace the team vision and work together to achieve it. The result is team members becoming interdependent, with particular strengths of individuals recognised and used to the benefit of the whole team and the pupils. Team members also support one another and just as the leader looks for opportunities to develop each member so members look for opportunities to develop other members and the team leader. This does not mean that there are never any disagreements. Open debate is encouraged and is one of the things that helps to clarify team values and the direction the team is going in. Team successes are celebrated publicly as are the achievements of individual team members. It is not unusual to hear laughter coming from meetings of successful teams. This indicates that a relaxed rapport has been achieved and is in no way at odds with a team's serious purpose.

4. *Open lines of communication*

Team members talk to one another about issues and there is an atmosphere in which positive and negative feedback can be given. People are open-minded to other people's arguments and new ideas are encouraged and debated. Individual team members are assertive but not aggressive and conflicting viewpoints are seen as normal. Indeed, lively debate is seen as a constructive feature of decision making. While lines of communication are open there are also clear procedures for holding meetings and making decisions.

5. Regular reviews of progress

Teams are not frightened of reviewing progress. Successes are celebrated and failures are analysed so as to build on good practice and avoid repeating mistakes. All team members are involved in development planning and target setting.

An effective team combines creativity and energy to produce an output greater than the sum of its parts – this is known as *synergy*. You may have experienced synergy as part of a team putting on a public performance such as a show or maybe during an OFSTED inspection. What probably sticks in your mind is the real sense of working together for a common goal. Synergy is what good team leaders try and create in the everyday work of their teams.

A quick mental checklist for making appraisals of team functioning is provided by Hardingham (1995) using the acronym PERFORM. This has been modified to suit a school context in Table 5.1.

Productivity	Is the team getting enough done? Is there evidence that the work being done is raising pupil achievement?
Empathy	Do the team members feel comfortable with one another? Do they encourage one another to succeed?
Roles and goals	Do they know what they're supposed to be doing?
Flexibility	Are they open to outside influence, willing regularly to review roles and keen to innovate?
Openness	Do they say what they think? Are meetings lively with plenty of debate?
Recognition	Do they praise one another and publicise achievement?
Morale	Do people want to be in this team? Do team members spread good cheer?
Common indicators of problems in these areas are:	
Productivity	A team leader in a bad temper; performance targets not met
Empathy	No coffee at team meetings; tension between members
Roles and goals	Puzzled faces in meetings; unfinished tasks
Flexibility	Annoyed outsiders talking about the 'fortress mentality'; failure to embrace new ideas; complacency
Openness	Silence in meetings
Recognition	Backbiting; jealousy; splinter groups
Morale	No laughter at meetings; everyone looking for new jobs; people clock-watching and religiously sticking to 1265 hours and contractual duties

Table 5.1 Effective team checklist

The team life-cycle

As well as understanding the difference between a team and a group, it is useful to understand the different stages that teams go through as they develop. Research has shown that these stages are fairly predictable.

- **Stage 1 – Forming**
  At this stage the newly created team is a group of people who are getting the measure of one another. They are concerned with 'who fits where'. Group members may exhibit self-conscious politeness, embarrassment, stilted communication or false enthusiasm.

- **Stage 2 – Storming**
  At this stage team members' different personalities and approaches to work can begin to clash. There is concern over 'how we work together' and a certain amount of 'juggling for position'. Group members may come into conflict and there is likely to be heated debate and discussion. Nevertheless, things begin to be achieved.

- **Stage 3 – Norming**
  At this stage the 'rules of the game' become clear and the members of the team begin to exhibit group behaviour. Goals are focused on effectively and a more relaxed and purposeful atmosphere emerges.

- **Stage 4 – Performing**
  The team now settles into a comfortable way of working and decisions and agreements are reached more easily. There is a feeling of confidence and achievement, with individuals in the team clear about roles and responsibilities.

With some teams in school these stages are easily recognised. Working parties, formed with a specific goal in mind, often follow this pattern. For established teams the cycle can be iterative, with teams switching between stages as they encounter new issues to resolve. In some ways the organisation of schools around the academic year, with the long summer break, encourages teams to make a fresh start each September, especially as there are usually some newly appointed colleagues joining teams at this point. It is important that middle managers create opportunities for newcomers to contribute to team activity so that norming is accomplished quickly. Sadly, some teams never seem to develop beyond the storming stage.

Newly appointed middle managers often feel quite vulnerable when taking over an established team. A team culture or ethos will already exist and some members will feel anxious and irritated by the prospect of the inevitable forming, storming and norming that will occur. New managers are likely to be compared with the team leaders they replace as new roles and ways of working evolve, making it a stressful time. It is important that new team leaders behave with tact and integrity and do not fall into the trap of feeling they have to dominate others in order to prove their leadership capabilities. As was noted in Chapter 4, a calm and professional approach is the way to earn respect from fellow team members.

Belbin's work on effective teams

Finding outstanding managers (see Chapter 2) is not easy. A single person cannot be all things to all people and rarely has all the qualities needed to be excellent in terms of both people and task management. Effective managers, therefore, draw upon the strengths of members of their teams to compensate for weakness they are aware of in themselves. The importance of using the strengths of all team members is summed up neatly in the phrase 'none of us is as smart as all of us'. Dr Belbin's (1981) work on team effectiveness is both fascinating and influential, providing useful insights into how *the whole can be greater than the sum of its parts.*

Through his work at the Management College, Henley, Dr Belbin learnt to recognise individuals who made a crucial difference to teams. He identified eight clear team-types and to these individuals he gave names. He went on to relate observed team behaviour to psychological traits, using psychometric tests. Dr Belbin and his colleagues then constructed balanced teams containing the eight identified team-types. When set management challenges the balanced teams consistently performed more effectively than teams with random membership. When there were fewer than eight team members then people tended to play more than one role, as necessary.

Belbin's work provides convincing evidence that getting team composition right can be as important as appointing the right individual to be leader. While it is not possible easily to change the composition of teams in schools, a consideration of the team-types that exist in any team may be a very fruitful starting point for analysing the reasons for the under-performance of a particular team. A consideration of Belbin's eight team-types should enable middle managers to recognise themselves and others in their teams. It is important to remember that the names Belbin chose are less important than the characteristics associated with them.

Chairman

Traits: stable, dominant, extrovert. S/he may not be the leader of the team so 'chairman' is a misleading term – but s/he certainly has team leadership qualities. The chairman:
- presides over the team and coordinates its efforts to meet targets;
- is intelligent but not brilliant and not an outstandingly creative thinker;
- has self-discipline and integrity;
- has good authority and is often charismatic;
- is not domineering but in control in a relaxed way;
- trusts people and is not jealous;
- recognises the strengths of others and uses them to create a team;
- is easy to talk to and a good listener;
- is a good communicator;
- is capable of making decisions once everyone has had their say.

Shaper

Traits: anxious, dominant, extrovert. S/he is likely to be the task leader, even if the chairman is the 'social leader'. The shaper:
- is full of nervous energy;
- is impulsive and impatient;
- becomes easily frustrated;
- often has rows but does not harbour grudges;
- tries to unite ideas into feasible projects;
- is self-confident on the outside but full of self-doubt;
- is competitive;
- is critical of vague and muddled thinking;
- is often perceived by other people as arrogant;
- can make a team feel uncomfortable but does make things happen.

Plant

Traits: dominant, high IQ, introvert. Belbin discovered that an ineffective team could be improved by 'planting' one of this type in it. A plant:
- is full of original ideas and proposals;
- is very imaginative in solving problems;
- is more concerned with major issues than detail;
- even though introverted is forceful and uninhibited;
- can be prickly and critical of the ideas of others;
- is bad at accepting criticism of own ideas.

Monitor evaluator

Traits: high IQ, stable, introvert. Likely to be serious and not very exciting – main contribution is dispassionate analysis rather than creative ideas – s/he will stop the team embarking on misguided projects. The monitor evaluator:
- is a constructive critic and clear thinker;
- is not highly motivated;
- is slow to reach a decision;
- can assimilate and interpret large volumes of complex written material;
- can be tactless when assessing the judgements of others;
- can lower team morale by being a damper;
- is dependable but lacks warmth;
- offers judgment that is rarely wrong.

Implementer

Traits: stable and controlled, a practical organiser who turns the team's plans into manageable tasks. The company worker:
- sorts out objectives;
- is logical;
- is disciplined;
- has integrity;
- doesn't like rapidly changing situations;
- is very well organised;
- is efficient and systematic;
- can be over-competitive;
- always understands policies and knows what should be being done.

Resource investigator

Traits: stable, dominant, extrovert. A very likeable member of the team – relaxed, sociable and enthusiastic. The resource investigator:
- tends to drop ideas as quickly as they are taken up;
- gathers information from outside the team;
- makes friends easily;
- is diplomatic;
- is quick to see the relevance of the ideas of others;
- is ineffective without the stimulus of others;
- is good under pressure but over relaxes when it eases.

Team worker

Traits: stable, extrovert, low in dominance – very aware of the feelings and needs of team members and senses emotional undercurrents – helps to keep team morale up in a low key way. The team worker:
- knows about the private lives of team members;
- is popular and likeable;
- is a good communicator and listener;
- is loyal and supportive;
- promotes unity;
- dislikes friction and personal confrontation;
- is uncompetitive;
- helps team unity;
- works behind the scenes to keep peace.

Finisher

Traits: anxious, introvert – the finisher worries about what might go wrong and checks details almost obsessively. The finisher:
- communicates sense of urgency to others;
- exerts good self-control;
- is intolerant towards casual members of the team;
- is compulsive about meeting deadlines;
- can lower morale of team by spreading anxiety;
- can miss the bigger picture by concentrating on detail.

In recent years Belbin has modified role titles and identified one extra role (Belbin 1993). These changes are summarised in Table 5.2.

Middle managers in schools could probably recognise the behaviour of members of their teams from the points above and it would

Title	Role	Characteristic
Chairperson	Coordinating	Calm, self-confident
Shaper	Team leading	Highly strung, 'driven'
Plant	Innovating	Thinker, innovator, individualistic
Monitor-evaluator	Critical thinking	Sober, unemotional, able to assess, judge and evaluate
Implementer	Getting work done	Practical, common sense, organising ability
Team worker	Personal relationships	Socially orientated, responds well to people
Completer	Keeping group on its toes	Orderly, painstaking, determined
Resource investigator	Keeping in touch with people outside the organisation	Extrovert, wide contacts, likes making links
Specialist	Providing knowledge and skills in rare supply	Single minded, self-starting, dedicated

Table 5.2 Belbin's team roles

probably be beneficial, given the right team ethos, to conduct a fuller assessment of team members as a team development exercise. The important thing is that people identified as being a certain team-type should feel neither inferior nor superior as a result. For success, there is a critical role for each team-type and middle managers should ensure colleagues are used appropriately. If teams are assessed and appear unbalanced in terms of the range of team-types identified then this should to be discussed openly. Knowledge is power and although people can't change their personalities they can modify behaviour associated with their personality, if this is necessary to improve team performance. Clearly, any attempt to use Belbin's ideas would need to be handled with great sensitivity and it would be unwise for a newly appointed middle manager to look to Belbin as a panacea for problems being encountered with team behaviour. However, an established team, led by a self-critical and respected middle manager, might well be able to use Belbin's ideas as a way of gaining both individual self-knowledge and becoming a more effective team.

What can go wrong with teams?

All kinds of things can go wrong with teams. Team leaders will only improve team ethos and performance by reflecting honestly and critically on the behaviour of their team. A good starting point is to consider your own behaviour – a good team leader usually manages to produce an effective team; a poor team leader usually blames other team members when things are going badly.

Meetings

For many people 'teamwork' and meetings go hand in hand. It is important to realise that meetings can easily wreck, rather than build, teams if they are unnecessary, unproductive and badly managed. Chapter 7 offers advice on how to ensure meetings are effective, but it is worth mentioning at this point that the manager is not automatically the best person to chair every team meeting. It is true that most people assume the manager will chair team meetings because being the chairman goes with the role. However, there may be occasions when another member of the team acts as chairman, enabling the manager to become one among equals. This is one practical way of encouraging both collegiality and staff development. Whoever chairs a meeting, it is important to ensure that 'action points' are recorded, with named individuals clear about what they have agreed to do and by when.

Conflict

Conflict in teams can occur in situations where there is rivalry between colleagues or fundamental differences of philosophy. Conflict associated with the 'storming' stage of team development is likely to pass, but if conflict is sustained, repetitive and hurtful to individuals it will undermine the team and prevent the growth of a collaborative team culture. This kind of conflict is quite different from the healthy debate and exchange of ideas associated with dynamic teams. Sometimes conflict can result from personality clashes, where two team members dislike each other intensely. This kind of temperamental incompatibility is best dealt with by speaking to each individual separately about the problem to see what ways forward they suggest. Defining their roles clearly can also help, as can praising each one for the particular strengths they bring to the team.

Complacency

In some teams there is little or no debate, little reflection and much defensiveness against criticism or challenge. Such groups have convinced themselves that the team is always right and are only shaken from their complacency by something like a damning OFSTED report. It is most likely that such teams have seen little movement of staff over the years and have not been challenged by senior managers through the appraisal process and target setting. Complacency is a dangerous thing and this is one reason why appointing a new middle manager from outside the school in some circumstances makes more sense than promoting someone from within the team. A new manager joining such a team would need to work hard to change the culture and should not, in the short term, worry too much if team members seem nostalgic about the team they have lost.

Techniques which help teams to develop and succeed

Treating team members decently, as outlined in Chapter 4, is important for getting the most out of individuals. However, as we have seen in this chapter, a team is more than the sum of its parts and there are certain practical devices which can assist in getting group members working as a team.

Brainstorming

Most teachers are aware of brainstorming – the generation of as many ideas as quickly as possible by a group of people – and many teachers use the technique effectively in their teaching. Brainstorming can be a useful team building tool because it can be fun, it encourages contributions from all team members and it creates the kind of 'clean communication' which helps teams to become dynamic and creative. When a brainstorm goes well it builds confidence and gives a team a real sense of achievement. Brainstorming sessions are especially useful for helping to integrate newly appointed colleagues into a team. If brainstorms are to be successful it is important to remember that every idea is recorded; no idea is evaluated at the brainstorm stage and the team leader does not have to be the scribe.

The PEP talk

PEP stands for 'Planning Effective Performance'. It consists of three simple questions: What did we do that worked well? What did we do that didn't work well? What shall we do next time? PEP talks should focus on moving forward and should avoid recriminations. PEP talks can be long or short depending on the event or issue under review. They can be used to evaluate almost any team activity: field trips, PSA (Parent Staff Association) events and concerts are just three examples. Of course, it is vital that, having engaged a team in the PEP talk process, conclusions reached are acted upon. If they are not then people will simply become cynical and put no real effort into the process when it is used again.

Development plans and action plans

Development planning is now well established in schools and the cycle of *audit–plan–implement–review* is used with varying degrees of success. A more detailed exploration of managing development is provided in Chapter 9, the important point to make at this stage is that development planning must be a collective activity. Sharing views about what has been achieved and deciding together on objectives, individual responsibilities and success criteria is crucial to team effectiveness. It is also vital if teachers are to feel both empowerment and accountability.

Self-assessment and reflection

As a middle manager it is important to reflect on your capacity for creating an effective team. Included below are a number of scaled questions which should help you identify your strengths and weaknesses. These questions are based loosely on a series of questions by Maddux (1986) and modified to suit a school context. Circle the number that best reflects where you fall on the scale. The higher the number, the more the characteristic describes you. When you have finished total the numbers circled and look at the comment that goes with your score. Don't despair if your attitudes have generated negative comments. The important thing is to plan to modify your behaviour so that you are doing all you can to create an effective team.

If I could appoint a new member of my team I would select someone with good interpersonal skills ahead of someone with excellent academic qualifications.	7 6 5 4 3 2 1
I help my team develop a sense of ownership by involving them in problem solving, policy writing and goal setting.	7 6 5 4 3 2 1
I try to provide team spirit by encouraging colleagues to work with new team members on certain tasks.	7 6 5 4 3 2 1
I talk to people openly and honestly and encourage the same kind of communication in return.	7 6 5 4 3 2 1
I always try to keep my word. If I have promised a colleague something I always deliver because their trust is important to me.	7 6 5 4 3 2 1
I use activities such as brainstorms with my team as a means of generating trust and respect between team members.	7 6 5 4 3 2 1
I try to use directing, coaching, supporting and delegating as appropriate to individual team members.	7 6 5 4 3 2 1
I understand that conflict within groups is normal, but work to resolve it quickly and fairly before it can become destructive.	7 6 5 4 3 2 1
I believe people perform as a team when they know what is expected and what the benefits are.	7 6 5 4 3 2 1
I am not frightened of tackling team members who under-perform.	7 6 5 4 3 2 1

What your score indicates

- A score between 60 and 70 indicates a positive attitude towards colleagues and the type of attitude needed to build and maintain a strong team. You appear to be an empowering leader, capable of raising and maintaining morale.
- A score between 40 and 59 is acceptable and with reasonable effort you should be able to lead an effective team. Even so, you

should think carefully about your approach. Are there ways in which you can be even more positive with members of your team?

- A score below 40 means you need to examine your behaviour towards colleagues and reflect critically on your management philosophy. Do you praise enough? Do you empower? Do you act with integrity? Do you recognise the need to team build? Are you publicly enthusiastic?

Summary

A team is more than a group of people placed together because they have some aspect of their work in common. A team is characterised by:

- members sharing a vision;
- members being interdependent;
- members knowing what the team's goals are;
- members understanding what their unique contribution to achieving the goals is;
- members communicating openly;
- members supporting and trusting one another;
- healthy debate between members;
- relaxed but purposeful relationships.

A successful team is creative and flexible and the achievements of the team are greater than the achievements of individuals in the team working separately would be. A successful team is likely to be led by a manager who encourages collaboration and empowerment, who trusts and praises individuals in the team and who is receptive to new ideas and opportunities.

The greatest threats to team effectiveness are unproductive meetings, rivalry between team members, personality clashes and complacency. Middle managers can encourage teamwork through the use of collaborative communication devices such as brainstorms, PEPs and collective development planning.

CHAPTER SIX

Effective Communication

Introduction

Communication is an activity which takes place when a message is transferred satisfactorily from one party to another. For communication to take place there has to be a source, transmission through channels and a receiver. Middle managers have to communicate with a wide range of client groups and need to make their chosen style and language (spoken or written) *fit for purpose*. The Teacher Training Agency spells out the need for effective communication by stating that subject leaders should have 'the ability to make points clearly and understand the views of others' (TTA 1998). This phrase is useful as it reminds us that communication should be a two-way exchange; negotiation in communication is often vital if the message is to be fully received, accepted by the parties concerned and acted upon.

Poor communication lies at the heart of many misunderstandings and disputes that arise in primary schools. Even in teams that have cultivated a positive ethos and where collaboration is well established, team leaders often have to make decisions 'on the hoof' and failure to inform colleagues of these can cause resentment. Occasional failures of communication will be tolerated if the foundation stones of good management are in place, but when poor communication becomes habitual it can undermine good team relationships. In other teams it can be the failure to communicate clearly and effectively which is the barrier to creating a sharing and supportive team culture. In teams where comments like 'I always seem to be the last person to find out what's going on in this school' and 'what exactly are we doing before the next team meeting then?' there is clearly cause for concern.

One problem is that communication skills are frequently taken for granted. It is assumed that colleagues who speak the same language need only the time, effort and sincerity to communicate successfully. As communication is a fundamental teaching tool newly appointed managers often feel that they don't need to develop this skill. This is not usually the case and managers need to analyse and reflect on their communication skills as on all other aspects of management. Just as teachers refine their classroom style over the years so team leaders learn how to communicate with greater proficiency as they become more experienced. If you are a prospective or newly appointed middle manager this chapter should help you to avoid making basic mistakes with communication and thus help you to establish yourself more smoothly in a management role.

Middle managers and communication networks

Middle managers operate extensive communication networks. A typical communication network for a year leader or subject coordinator is shown Table 6.1. It will be slightly different for other middle managers.

As a middle manager you do not have to communicate actively with all the groups all the time, but you should be aware of the range of

Daily communication	Regular communication	Occasional communication
Colleagues	Head teacher	Members of parent-teacher association
Members of your team	Deputy headteacher	
Pupils in your class and other classes	Other middle managers	HE tutors of students on ITT
Non-teaching support staff	Governors	Teachers in other primary schools
(Students on ITT)	Parents	Teachers in infant and secondary schools
		Local community leaders
		Local industry
		HMI
		OFSTED
		LEA advisers and inspectors
		The media
		Past pupils

Formality of communication increases →

Table 6.1 Communication network of a middle manager

'client groups' you may have to make contact with. Generally speaking communication will be more formal with people in the 'Occasional' category than with people in the 'Daily' category. However, there may be exceptions to this rule: regular contact with colleagues in other schools may result in a healthy and relaxed approach to communication, for example. Also, much will depend on the personalities of the particular people in each group. There may be some people who change categories over time. For example, students on ITT may need to be seen every day in the early stages of their training but less regularly as their skill levels develop.

Networking, the activity of developing personal contacts, is endemic to organisations. It can be useful for middle managers in primary schools to share information, ideas and concerns with colleagues in similar management roles from their own school and other schools. Being aware of what other subject coordinators think about a particular policy proposal that will impact on your role as subject leader is perfectly legitimate, for example. Middle managers need to be aware, though, that by identifying with a particular group there may be negative side effects, especially in schools which have not developed a shared sense of purpose and collaborative ways of working. In such schools certain groups may not be supportive of the head teacher's vision for the school. Circles of people discussing issues in hushed tones is undesirable and runs counter to a culture of openness and collaboration.

Making communication effective

Effective communication is more likely to occur in collaborative school cultures, where people are valued, encouraged to voice their opinions and supported than in hierarchical institutions. When people feel trusted, secure and confident they are much more likely to admit to not understanding messages given or to engage in debate as a means of achieving agreed meanings. In more rigid teams and schools a climate of closed communication is likely to exist, with greater competition between team members and control maintained in part through suppression of information. Two contrasting communication climates are outlined in Table 6.2.

There are various communication flows which exist within institutions and teams (Lewis 1975). Two contrasting arrangements are the chain and the all-channel model illustrated in Figure 6.1. The chain is associated with hierarchical cultures with a line-management approach. Communication tends to be instructional, which can work

Open communication climate	Closed communication climate
Communication encourages and values everyone, regardless of status	Communication emphasises differences in status
Communication shows empathy and understanding	Communication is impersonal
Feedback and debate are encouraged	Little discussion is allowed
There is a focus on collective problem solving	Decisions are made by a few who hold positions of power
Statements are informative not evaluative	Statements are judgemental
Error is recognised and minimised	People are blamed
There are no hidden messages	Messages hold hidden meaning

Table 6.2 Communication climates

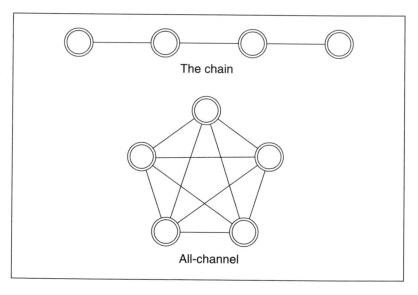

Figure 6.1 Contrasting communication flows

with simple tasks, but morale tends to be low at the end of the chain. The all-channel model seems most effective for complex tasks and would be the favoured approach of managers wanting to generate a collaborative culture in which the views of professionals are encouraged and valued.

Encouraging an open communication climate in your team is important and the team meeting is the obvious place for the all-channel model to be encouraged.

Effective communication involves making appropriate use of a variety of communication techniques: formal, informal, oral and written – *fitness for purpose* is the important thing. It is essential that the people you communicate with feel that your choice of method is appropriate; this means being sensitive to people's needs. Two examples will illustrate this point.

- **Example 1**

   A Key Stage Coordinator has been asked to approach a member of her team over the fact that he may have to change the room he will have as his classroom next year and she knows that this might not please him. Because she is busy, she decides to inform him about what could happen next year via a quick memo. The information is communicated, but not in the right way. In this instance the Key Stage Coordinator should have made time to meet with the team member and discuss the matter with him personally.

- **Example 2**

   A Music Coordinator receives a letter from a parent about an incident in band practice that the parent would like to discuss with him as soon as possible. He sends a quick verbal message back via the pupil concerned saying that he will be in touch soon. This is an inappropriate response, which will reflect badly on the school. The parent deserved a telephone call or a more formal written reply. It is not unreasonable for the Coordinator to delay a meeting, but the method used to communicate this was unprofessional.

Verbal communication skills

Most communication is verbal and this is theoretically a very efficient form of communication, allowing the transmission of complex information from one person to another. Thoughtful and reflective managers can get the basics of this form of communication right by thinking about their listening and speaking, social skills and how best to create understanding.

Listening and speaking

Listening requires an awareness of bias, visual signals and vocal sounds.

1. **Bias** Everyone's point of view includes bias of some kind. Being aware of this should help to prevent managers from dismissing the views of others too readily. It is important not to make assumptions about the likely views of colleagues and so pre-judge their ideas or arguments. By being open-minded and encouraging a range of ideas team leaders help to generate trust, real debate and collaboration from their team.

2. **Visual signals** A visual sign is body language. People interpret the meaning of body language according to their own understanding, usually based on background, upbringing and experience. Even so, appropriate gestures can add considerable meaning to communication. Listening is obviously enhanced when eye contact is made with the speaker and people will be encouraged to contribute when they can see they have the full attention of the listener. A body turned away from a speaker is very discouraging, for example.

3. **Vocal sounds** Listening to the sound and tone of a speaker's voice enhances understanding. Sometimes there are hidden meanings which can be read from the tone being used. Speakers signal an emotional state through their voice more than their choice of words and it is important for a manager to tune in to the message being conveyed.

Speaking effectively requires tuning in to the listener's needs and pacing what is said accordingly. It is important for managers to speak *to* people not *at* them. This means giving people the opportunity to respond to statements made so that a dialogue can take place. Speakers communicate warmth, interest and authority through their voice and those who vary their tone and rhythm are usually more engaging and interesting than those who don't. Humour in tone and content is a good way to relax people and need not detract from serious points you are trying to make.

Social skills

Socially skilled information exchange occurs when the leader:
- has clear goals to be achieved through the communication;
- behaves in a way that conveys a consistent overall impression; eye

contact, facial expression, tone of voice and body language support the message being given in words;
- chooses an appropriate time and situation to convey the message.

Creating understanding

It is the leader's responsibility to open a debate, encourage colleagues' contributions and guide discussion so that a common understanding emerges within the group. This enhances a group's sense of purpose and clarifies the team vision.

Newly appointed managers can feel threatened when difficult issues are discussed and team members present their opinions forcefully, especially if there appears to be opposition to the views presented by the manager. Leaders committed to encouraging a collaborative culture turn such discussions to their advantage by attentive listening and setting a tone of tolerant discussion. Respect generates respect and it is a manager's duty to set the right tone. The key task is to achieve a balance between creative exchange of views and a free-for-all where the loudest voice gets heard most. Managing meetings is covered in more detail in Chapter 7 but at this point it is worth mentioning three important skills which managers should develop in order to facilitate effective group discussions.

1. Managers must insist that people speak one at a time through the chairman. This prevents the loudest and most confident team members dominating discussions and encourages the participation of everybody.
2. The leader must learn to keep a discussion on track. If there is too much digression from the main point then the leader should paraphrase what has just been said, making links to the key issue under discussion. This should be done in a non-judgemental manner so as not to discourage the colleague responsible for the digression. A good example of when to use this technique is when teachers introduce long anecdotes about particular pupils they have taught to illustrate discussion points.
3. Team leaders need to be willing to intervene if two or more colleagues become locked in a dispute. The leader's task is to take attention away from the disputing participants and focus on the issues which they raised. Encouraging the rest of the group to discuss the controversial issue in order to find a solution best does this. Changing the subject is not a good strategy as it leaves the issue unresolved and likely to flare up again at some point in the future.

Barriers to effective verbal communication

Communication is ineffective when the receiver ends up with a different understanding from that intended by the transmitter of the message. This can be caused by poor communication skills on the part of the sender but barriers to effective communication also arise as a result of a climate of mistrust. For example, if managers make a habit of saying one thing but doing another it should not be surprising if their messages cease to be accepted at face value.

The most common barriers to communication are semantics, status, cultural and gender differences, and information overload.

Semantics

Different words have different meanings and words can be interpreted differently by different people. Thus it is important that everybody uses the same definitions. In whole staff and team meetings this means discussing what words mean, especially important when issues such as racist behaviour and harassment are being debated. Parents sometimes need to have words that are used regularly by teachers explained to them – the difference between SATs tests and tasks, for example.

Status

In schools that are hierarchical status can become a barrier to effective communication. Junior colleagues can feel reluctant to ask for clarification if a communication is unclear because they fear looking stupid in the eyes of older and more senior colleagues. This is one reason why it is necessary to build an ethos of trust and support in a team which means no one is ever embarrassed to admit they don't understand something.

Cultural and gender differences

If managers are insensitive to differences of interpretation of words and non-verbal signals that can result from gender or cultural differences they will not be effective communicators. Putting people at their ease is necessary if a relaxed team ethos is to be built; this means team members being sensitive to the feelings and expectations of others. Physical contact is an example of behaviour which can produce very positive or very negative responses depending on the interpretation attached to it. The manager must set the tone by getting to know each team member individually and by showing appropriate respect and sensitivity.

Information overload

When the timing and content of a communication is inappropriate people may fail to act on it. Even loyal and hard working colleagues reach saturation point and are unable to take more information on board. Too many items on the agenda of a team meeting can result in information overload, for example.

The importance of being assertive

Much has been made in this book so far of the need to encourage collaboration and openness in your team and in this chapter open communication has been advocated. In teams where members trust and support one another people are encouraged to be assertive. Being assertive means taking responsibility for our behaviour, having respect for ourselves and others and being honest. It allows us to say what we want or feel but not at other people's expense. It means understanding the point of view of other people and being self-confident and positive. It is not about winning come what may or getting our own way all of the time. Assertiveness is about handling conflict and coming to an acceptable compromise.

At some stage middle managers are sure to encounter people who are aggressive and people who are passive. Being aggressive means getting your own way at the expense of others and making them feel worthless or incompetent. Being passive means ignoring your interests and allowing others to manipulate you by denying how you really think or feel. It is important that middle managers are neither aggressive nor passive and that they encourage assertiveness in other team members. Not only is this morally right but it creates a stronger, more dynamic and more able team and ensures that honest communication occurs. Middle managers should learn to recognise passive, assertive and aggressive behaviour in order to be able to respond appropriately (see Table 6.3).

It is especially important to recognise signs of aggression when dealing with angry parents. Responding inappropriately to these signs could be potentially dangerous. How we listen, how we respond and our body language can help us to diffuse conflict situations. Whenever a parent, colleague or pupil has what they regard as a grievance it is

	Passive	Assertive	Aggressive
Verbal content	• Rambling • Apologies • Self put-downs • Frequent justifications	• Clear statements • Distinctions between fact and opinion • Questions to find out opinions of others • Ways of resolving problems	• Boastfulness • Opinions expressed as fact • Threats • Blame put on others • Sarcasm
Voice and speech	• Wobbly • Soft • Monotone • Pauses • Frequent throat clearing	• Steady • Rich and warm • Clear • Fluent • Emphasises key words	• Very firm • Cold • Strident • Loud • Abrupt • Emphasises blaming words
Face and eyes	• Evasive • Looking down	• Smiles when pleased • Frowns when angry • Firm eye contact	• Scowls • Eyebrows raised in amazement • Tries to stare-down
Body language	• Arms crossed (protection) • Hand-wringing • Shrugs • Mouth covered	• Open hand movements • Sits upright but relaxed • Stands with head held up	• Finger pointing • Fist thumping • Sits upright • Stands tall • Strides around • Arms crossed

Table 6.3 Passive, assertive and aggressive behaviour

important to listen, show understanding and ask questions. If you feel their anger is misguided it is tempting to state your position firmly but it would be wrong to do this when they are full of anger. By listening and showing empathy a dangerous situation can be diffused; there will be opportunities to explain your position later. By avoiding aggressive body language yourself you help to calm the anger in others.

This does not mean you have to 'give in' to unreasonable people. Your aim will be to come to a joint agreement on action and this is more likely to be achieved by allowing a person who is 'worked up' to have their say first. Once an angry person has calmed down and you have convinced them of your concern and sincerity things can begin to move forward. It is important that any grievance is fully investigated and, once the facts are known, your position can be stated firmly and an appropriate way forward negotiated with the parent (or colleague or pupil) concerned. The important thing is that by using appropriate communication skills in a heated situation you have prevented an escalation of anger into violence. Remember, listening shows cooperation, showing understanding indicates you care and asking questions allows you to gain control. Good teachers use these techniques with pupils and effective managers use them also.

Written communication

Middle managers in schools need to be able to communicate clearly in writing. They are accountable to a range of different client groups and need to think carefully about the needs and expectations of the audience they are communicating with. As with many other areas of management *fitness for purpose* is the important consideration: a memo to a colleague will clearly be written in a very different style from a report for governors, for example.

Middle managers are usually involved with communicating in writing with the various groups listed in Table 6.1. The range of documents they will have to prepare will include: worksheets and booklets for pupils; memos and minutes for colleagues; reports for senior staff and governors; progress reports for pupils and parents; a subject policy; schemes of work; development plans and targets; materials promoting events; and a range of letters to parents and others. Good word processing skills are essential as the use of a computer is bound to save you time, even if you have some degree of secretarial support for producing documents.

The tools of written communication are sound grammar, accurate spelling, structure and punctuation. In formal documents each sentence needs to be effective and it makes sense to use the following steps: pre-writing; drafting; revising; editing; printing.

1. **Pre-writing** This stage involves the gathering of ideas, such as by brainstorming a series of developments chronologically or listing the advantages and disadvantages of a particular proposal.
2. **Drafting** This stage involves the initial production of the document. You need to focus and structure the ideas you generated in pre-writing into an order and format that will make sense for your chosen audience.
3. **Revising** This involves reading your document carefully to determine whether it delivers its intended message for its intended audience. At this stage you may add new material, delete inappropriate material and rearrange the order of information to achieve maximum effect.

4. **Editing** You now need to check spelling, grammar, punctuation and tone to ensure that the finished document is accurate and polished.
5. **Printing** Ensure that the finished product looks good by using a laser printer or good ink jet printer. Ensure that pages are numbered and that the front cover does justice to the contents. It is a good idea for a school to develop a 'house-style' in order to market itself both internally and externally (see next section).

Communication and marketing

Many teachers still feel that marketing has little to do with teaching. They associate marketing with the commercial world and with persuading people, often by exaggerated claims, to part with their money. Marketing, they feel, is *gloss at the expense of substance*. If schools see marketing simply as *promotion* then there is a real danger that their marketing will simply become an 'add on' and that their glossy brochures will bear little resemblance to the reality of everyday school life. However, schools are increasingly competing for pupils and it is important that they generate a positive image by communicating their strengths and achievements effectively.

Many schools go further with marketing, though, seeing it as an integral part of the management process and using marketing to help with quality assurance. Marketing in such schools is characterised by the following attitudes.

Marketing is more than promotion

Marketing is seen as a process not an event. The clients (mainly pupils and parents) are involved in the process. They are asked their views about the quality of services provided through market research and their opinions are taken into account when planning for improvement. In such schools it is quite normal for pupils to be consulted through questionnaires and interviews about curriculum topics and preferred teaching and learning styles. The schools try to focus on the services they provide through the eyes of the users rather than simply as providers, in an effort to improve quality and satisfaction. Marketing is not an 'add on', it is part of the continuous process of school improvement. At its heart lies a desire to provide education of the highest quality.

Marketing is internal as well as external

Marketing is traditionally associated with conveying the right image to those outside the organisation. In the case of schools this means prospective pupils and parents, the local community, prospective staff, the LEA, OFSTED and so on. Schools taking marketing seriously realise that communicating effectively with internal clients is equally important. This doesn't just mean existing parents but includes current staff, pupils, governors and any regular visitors or helpers. Promoting the achievements of pupils and staff and 'talking up' the school is done continually and helps to maintain a positive ethos and a feeling of success.

In order to communicate an effective image staff (teaching and others) and governors must have a 'corporate perspective' and this means being clear about the mission and goals of the school. This is why some schools spend much time on developing a coherent vision for the school, agreeing its aims and values and making sure these are reflected in development plans before producing marketing materials. There is little point trying to promote a product which is ill defined or the suppliers have no faith in; this is why it is vital to create a shared school vision as the foundation for school development and marketing. It is worth noting that Sammons *et al.* (1995) found shared vision and goals to be a key characteristic of effective schools in the work they undertook for OFSTED.

Marketing is everyone's job

Even though a senior member of staff may be the marketing coordinator it is important that everyone working in a school sees marketing as their job. The way a receptionist welcomes visitors or a lunchtime supervisor handles children and the manner in which a teacher handles a complaint from a parent are all aspects of marketing. Indeed, a single incident badly handled can undo much that has been achieved in creating a positive image of a school. It is easy to see that an ineffective teacher will have much more impact on parents' likelihood of praising the school to the local community than glossy publicity leaflets. Ensuring a good standard of teaching and treating pupils and parents with respect should be modelled to others by middle managers at all times.

Appearance is important

The appearance of the school grounds and buildings creates a striking first impression. All staff need to be aware of the importance of encouraging children not to drop litter and to care for the school environment. Inside a school the reception area is very important. It should be inviting and friendly, with pupils' work displayed together with certificates and newspaper cuttings of pupils' and school achievements and awards. Beyond the reception area the appearance of classrooms says so much about the work of the school. Good primary teachers put their secondary colleagues to shame when it comes to the quality of displays, and effective middle managers need to keep an eye on this aspect of their team's work, while modelling good practice through their own displays. Finally, it is important to remember that people will make judgements about a school based on the appearance of its teachers, and all staff should be encouraged to create a professional impression through their dress and manner.

Reflection on marketing

Middle managers will be influenced in marketing by the school marketing policy. For example, in some schools teachers are free to make contacts with the local media whereas in others they must go through the marketing coordinator. Whatever policy is in operation the following questions are worth asking. They are not in any order of priority and the list is not an exhaustive one. Nevertheless, middle managers should raise awareness of the numerous ways in which an image of themselves and their team is being created and ways in which their work could be more 'client focused'.

- Does the way I deal with colleagues beyond my immediate team reflect well on my team and me?
- Do my memos create a professional image for me and my team? Do we have a 'team style'?
- Do I take enough care with the appearance and content of documents I produce for people?
- Do the display boards in my area create a good impression of the work of my team and their classes?
- Does the work of my team reflect the school mission?
- Do we produce accessible and interesting curriculum guides for parents, especially when we are asking for their support with aspects of the children's work?

- Do we use flyers, posters and newsletters to promote the work and achievements of my team?
- Do we involve pupils in evaluating topics and approaches?
- Do we use pupils to promote the school to visitors and parents?
- Do we make use of the local media in promoting the newsworthy things we are engaged in?
- Do I keep the head teacher informed about all the good things colleagues in my team are engaged in?
- Do I use team meetings and staff briefings as opportunities to celebrate achievements and praise the work of colleagues in my team?
- Do we praise pupils enough and do we publicise achievements of pupils in our area more widely, for example through assemblies?
- Are we welcoming to visitors?
- Do we create a good impression on parents' evenings?
- Are letters and reports to parents of a high enough standard?
- Do we listen to our pupils?
- Are we accessible to parents on a daily basis?
- Do I take parents' concerns seriously?
- Does the appearance of my classroom create a good impression?

It may be that you are the leader of a team providing a very good education to the pupils in your school but are not sharing your achievements with others. It is just as important not to be shy about announcing the achievements of your team as it is not to exaggerate their successes and make false claims. Informing others of the successes of staff and pupils in your area is important for several reasons:

- As a middle manager you should be keeping the head teacher informed of developments in your team. Heads need to know what colleagues are doing so that when they evaluate their performance or write references a clear picture exists.
- The public praising of colleagues for their successes raises self-esteem and increases motivation.
- The public praising of pupils for their successes raises self-esteem and increases motivation
- The public sharing of the achievements of one team in school can encourage other teams to reflect on their own achievements.
- It is important that all pupils and parents know about the successes of their school even if they are not directly involved. This increases confidence in the institution and is good marketing.

Reflections on school documents

Over the past two decades schools have been made increasingly accountable and middle managers need to ensure that they can provide a range of stakeholders with information they might require. In most schools there will be agreements about what information needs to be held at team level and which needs to be lodged with senior managers. If you are the relevant post holder could you answer 'yes' to the following questions?

- If a new pupil arrived from abroad would you be able to provide her parents with written information about your year group and about the curriculum she would be following? Would you be able to provide schemes of work that would help the pupil and her parents to understand how you were applying the National Curriculum and see clearly what work had been missed?
- If a Local Education Authority inspector arrived in school and wanted to see information about the subject you coordinate would you be able to provide it? Is your subject information/literature up-to-date? Do you have a staffing structure/responsibilities diagram in it? Have you got relevant timetable information available? Is your subject development plan up-to-date, including an indication of progress made with targets since they were set? Are you able to demonstrate value-added in your subject?
- If a parent wanted to know how her son was doing academically would you be able to show her? Does a portfolio of his work exist? Are you able to show how he is doing compared with national expectations for pupils of his age? Are you able to show how he is doing compared with other pupils in your class and school? Are you able to demonstrate progress being made over time, especially since the last end of key stage assessment?

Documents relating to all of the above ought to exist. If they don't then planning for their introduction ought to become part of your development plan. It is likely that assessment is handled as a whole-school issue and that models for demonstrating value-added or comparing performance are organised by a senior member of staff. Even so, the data generated ought to be with year and subject leaders, as their teams needs to consider it when planning for future improvements in performance.

It is not necessary to go over the top with documents. Some schools have beautifully produced, detailed documents which are more gloss than substance and do not reflect what is really happening in the school. Quality in the classroom from all teachers should be a school's primary aim. Clear planning, agreed schemes of work and systematic assessment procedures are important foundations of quality in the classroom. Documents for internal use relating to these areas must be in place. However, schools must also have a range of documents to meet the needs of clients. An up-to-date prospectus, a leaflet or flyer promoting aspects of the curriculum and a 'pupil-speak' version of relevant assessment criteria are essential. It does not have to be key post holders who produce all these. Tasks relating to documents can be agreed when the development plan is being written. Once in place, documents should be reviewed and updated annually.

Summary

Communication is central to the operation of an effective school and it is important that middle managers are skilled in communication techniques. An open and supportive team culture in which colleagues feel valued and secure is likely to promote open communication between members. Team leaders need to encourage new members to be honest and open by being clear and supportive in their own style of communication and by providing opportunities for newcomers to contribute and express their views.

Middle managers are involved in communicating with a wide range of people and must be able to adapt their style accordingly. Effective communication involves a range of strategies from informal discussions to formal written reports. Skilled communicators consider *fitness for purpose* when deciding which communication technique to employ. By seeing all people being communicated with as 'clients' (internal and external) team leaders begin to think about the need for clarity and quality in their communications. Considering what it would be like to be on the receiving end of their own communications is something middle managers need to do, however busy they may be.

Verbal and non-verbal communication involves listening and observing. Being a good listener is very important and encourages others to be open in their communication. As a middle manager you need to be assertive but not aggressive and you should encourage and develop assertiveness in your team members. If people feel both relaxed enough and confident enough to speak their minds a more dynamic team with shared and understood goals is likely to develop. This is far better than a passive team with no dynamism or a team that accepts what you say to your face but then moans and undermines your ideas behind your back.

As schools become increasingly self-sufficient and concerned about maintaining or improving their market position creating a positive image becomes a high priority. Middle managers have their part to play in this and should ensure that their communications reflect well on their teams and the school. By publicising the achievements of their team and their pupils middle managers are helping to market their area and the school and to contribute to raising morale. As well as producing quality material for school prospectuses, brochures, flyers and newsletters, middle managers need to be mindful that every interaction they engage in with colleagues, pupils, parents and others is an act of marketing. Pupils going home disgruntled and complaining to their parents because an incident has been handled badly can produce negative publicity which easily undermines the positive image being conveyed through the school's published materials.

CHAPTER SEVEN

Meetings

Introduction

Full staff meetings are likely to be a common feature of most primary schools. Other regular meetings may include staff who are part of a Key Stage, paired year group, year group and/or subject team. Other meetings may take place on an *ad hoc* basis. It is likely that the degree of formality with which meetings are conducted will increase with the size of the team involved. Thus in very large primary schools there may be a quite rigid approach to meetings, whereas in very small schools informal discussions at lunch breaks may well turn into unplanned meetings. Certainly, meetings are essential to the effective operation of any school or team but far too many take place that are unproductive or even dysfunctional. Newly appointed middle managers are all too aware that over the years they have attended many meetings which they regarded as a waste of time and which they were resentful of, given all the other things they could have done with the time. Organising successful meetings can be a demanding aspect of middle management and one that is sometimes a source of considerable stress to the inexperienced.

However, *effective* meetings have several advantages: they allow for clear communication; they improve staff skills in decision making; they provide a sense of involvement among team members, they improve job satisfaction; they increase commitment; and they ensure that managers and their teams are 'speaking the same language'. The essential thing is to make meetings productive. This chapter considers the factors and conditions that create successful meetings and provides some straightforward and pragmatic guidelines for ensuring your meetings are successful.

Why meet at all?

The number of meetings held in a school will reflect the size and culture of the school. In most schools a schedule of meetings is drawn up before the academic year commences to ensure that all teams are provided with fair and adequate meeting time within the 1265 hours of teachers' contracted time. This usually means having a rota of regular meetings. The advantage of this approach is that teams have regular scheduled meetings; the disadvantage is that there are some times in the year when meetings are not really needed and other times when additional meetings are needed because a team's workload is not evenly distributed throughout the year. For example, the Year 6 team will probably require additional meetings during the run up to the week of the SATs. Ideally, there should be a schedule of meetings, with team leaders empowered to decide whether or not it is necessary to meet rather than feeling obliged to meet because of 1265 hours.

In a team and a school with a collegiate approach to work, where colleagues feel valued and trusted, there is likely to be flexibility over meetings, with meetings that are additions to those identified on the schedule being called if necessary. The important phrase here is *if necessary*. When colleagues can see the need for a meeting and when the meeting is conducted in a way that produces clear outcomes there will be little resentment about attending. However, when people are forced to attend irrelevant and unproductive meetings simply because they are on a schedule, a '1265 mentality' can result in which teachers are unwilling to attend meetings not on the schedule. This mentality is associated with the Newtonian culture described in Chapter 2 and needs to be avoided at all costs.

If you decide to hold a meeting, do all members of your team need to attend? If you are considering major issues or are brainstorming new ideas on policy and philosophy the answer is clearly 'yes'. However, there is little point in all colleagues attending a meeting about a particular child's IEP if they are not and will not be involved in teaching that child. Thinking about the order of your agenda can help. By dealing with information-giving and whole-team issues first, you can involve all colleagues in the team; but then only those people connected with the agenda items which follow need remain. However, do bear in mind the points made about agenda writing given below.

Different types of meeting

If meetings are to be effective then all staff need to understand their function. Middle managers are required to plan, lead and participate in meetings which may have one or more of the following functions:

- to inform;
- to decide;
- to generate ideas;
- to problem-solve;
- to consult;
- to negotiate;
- to plan;
- to allocate;
- to motivate.

It is important to be clear about the purpose(s) of a meeting and the balance within it. For example, it would be inappropriate to use a sixty-minute meeting simply for information giving. Likewise, in a meeting devoted to generating ideas (strategic discussion) it would be unproductive to get bogged down in the minutiae of how a new policy might work in detail (operational discussion). Strategic discussions would be best kept to one meeting with operational considerations for another. In this way more will be achieved.

Steps to effective meetings

Before the meeting

1. Plan the meeting carefully by asking the following questions:
   - Who should attend?
   - What is the purpose of the meeting?
   - Where and when will it be held?
   - How many items will be on the agenda?
   - What briefing papers are needed?
2. Prepare and send out the agenda and briefing papers well in advance of the meeting (a week is usually fine). Think carefully about the agenda. You might want to deal with routine business first because only certain colleagues will then need to stay on to discuss later items which directly concern them. It is equally possible that you have a major issue to discuss that concerns everyone. Should this be the first item on the agenda? If it isn't then there is a danger that routine matters and announcements will use up valuable time needed for discussing the major issue,

unless the meeting is very tightly chaired. Ensure that there are not too many items on any one agenda; between three and five is usually a manageable number for a meeting of an hour. As team leader it is vital that you have prepared yourself for each item on the agenda so that you can provide clear thinking and answer any questions posed by the team.

3. Try to hold the meeting in a pleasant room and get there early to arrange the chairs. Different types of meeting work best with different seating arrangements (see p. 96) and so you must ensure that the seating is *fit for purpose*. Providing refreshments is always appreciated by colleagues and helps to set a relaxed tone, as well as preventing late arrivals using the excuse that they were desperate for a drink and had to wait for the kettle to boil! Don't time your after-school meetings to start immediately after teaching ends. Give people at least ten minutes to gather their thoughts. In some primary schools there is a culture of teachers being accessible to parents for brief exchanges of information at the end of the day and this needs to be taken into account in timing the start of meetings. A fifty minute meeting which begins promptly at 3.40 is likely to be more productive than a sixty minute meeting that is supposed to start at 3.30 but never does. A sloppy start to a meeting sets the wrong tone.

At the beginning of the meeting

1. Always start on time; this sets an appropriate business-like tone and means you are more likely to finish on time. Remember, there is no conflict between having a relaxed and collegiate team ethos and being business-like in meetings. People appreciate meetings that are run properly.

2. Clearly define roles within the meeting. Who is acting as chairperson, who is taking minutes and is anyone providing a specialist input? Although it is assumed that the team leader will be chairperson this doesn't have to be the case for every meeting. A team leader may wish to give a colleague the experience of running a meeting as part of their development, for example. If the meeting is a decision making meeting where a vote is being taken the team leader might think it fairer to allow a colleague to chair so that their own view can be expressed from the floor, with no danger of showing bias in the way the discussion is handled. It is a good idea to rotate minute writing as this spreads the work load, gives experience to newcomers and prevents the

chairperson of the meeting giving a particular 'flavour' to the decisions made. On a practical note, it is actually quite difficult for one person effectively to chair a meeting and make notes, however brief.

3. Review, revise and order the agenda. It may be that since the agenda was issued something urgent has occurred which needs addressing in preference to some routine items on the agenda, or a colleague who was due to contribute an item to the meeting may be ill, for example.

4. Remind colleagues of the time at which the meeting will end and, if necessary, remind them that there are time limits on certain agenda items. This helps to focus people's minds and, with effective chairing, prevents the meeting wandering off track.

5. Always review the action points from the previous meeting. If people are used to meetings being closed with clear action points and opened with a review of these it is more likely that they will be efficient in completing the action agreed. It also means that if action points have not been achieved some thought can be given to how best to move things forward. Being accountable to the team is an important aspect of the collegiate culture and being supported towards achieving goals is more likely if these goals are regularly reviewed.

6. If there are guests at your meeting or if you are chairing a meeting for the first time it is polite to ask all participants to introduce themselves. If you are chairing a one-off meeting it is important to ask all participants what they hope to get out of the meeting.

During the meeting

During the meeting the chairperson must adopt a style *fit for purpose* (see p. 95), but whatever the nature of the meeting it is important to:

- keep to time;
- keep people on-task;
- ensure action points are clear.

At the end of the meeting

1. Remind people of action points agreed upon during the meeting: who, what, when?

2. Set the date and time of the next meeting and develop a preliminary agenda. It might be that some non-essential items

from the current meeting have been deferred or that a team member is going on a course and needs an opportunity to report back at the next meeting.

3. Evaluate the meeting. This does not mean asking everyone to complete a questionnaire! It simply means giving people the chance to say whether or not they feel the aims of the meeting have been met. If people feel disgruntled that an issue has not been adequately debated it is better that they say so rather than leaving the meeting unhappy and uncommitted to a decision made.

4. Close the meeting crisply and positively. Generally, it is important to finish on time or even a few minutes early. However, on occasions members may decide to prolong a meeting by an agreed amount so as to get business finished or to prevent the need for another meeting. There is a big difference between meetings regularly over-running due to being badly chaired and an occasional meeting being extended due to unforeseen difficulties with a particular item. Remember, though, that for some colleagues extending a meeting may be very inconvenient as they might have other commitments to meet. It is not fair to exclude people from participation simply because they cannot alter their domestic arrangements at the drop of a hat.

5. Clean up the room and rearrange the furniture.

After the meeting

1. Liaise with the minute taker, if appropriate, to ensure that the minutes are accurate and efficiently written up and distributed (or made readily available in, for example, a file in the staffroom). With most colleagues you will simply need to thank them for taking the minutes but do nothing else, whereas with a new team member they may feel happier if you have seen the minutes before they are distributed or made available to other colleagues. Keep the minutes brief by reducing each item on the agenda to outcomes: the agreed action points – who, when and where? In some schools a standardised pro-forma for minutes exists and administrative staff type minutes of meetings up. This is an excellent idea for two reasons. First, a regular moan from teachers is that they do too much administration – here is one simple way a head teacher can be supportive in reducing administration. Second, minutes in a standardised form are easier for senior colleagues to digest and need contain only

essential information, namely the agreed action points but not unnecessary detail about who said what. In schools where no such arrangements exist middle managers would be advised to act together to explain the benefits of such a system to senior staff.

2. Monitor action points, as necessary, and begin to plan the next meeting. Some colleagues will not need to be reminded about what they have agreed to whereas others may benefit from questions on progress asked informally and others may need more overt support. As with so many other aspects of management, knowing your staff is essential and being flexible in your management style will pay dividends.

Some thoughts on chairing meetings

The success or failure of a meeting rests on how effectively the meeting is chaired. Usually, though not always, the team leader will be the person who chairs team meetings. The chairperson must fulfil a number of functions which make up the role. First, there is a leadership role. This involves setting guidelines, exercising authority, summarising discussions, insisting on facts before opinions and countering limited vision that can sometimes result from a group being well established and comfortable. Second, there is a gatekeeper role. This involves protecting the weak and vulnerable, encouraging the nervous, motivating the uninterested, controlling the dominant and managing ramblers and jokers. Third, there is a referee role which involves keeping cool, staying neutral and managing conflict while at the same time allowing healthy debate. Finally, there is an administrative role which involves organising the physical setting, keeping to time and ensuring notes are taken.

Effective chairing of meetings requires effective interpersonal skills. The chairperson must ensure that the atmosphere of the meeting is conducive to discussion and that members feel valued. Middle managers need to develop skills in managing teams during meetings. This means taking the lead, establishing acceptable behaviour and setting a good example. A sense of humour is useful for diffusing conflict in a meeting and careful planning should avoid many problems. A middle manager who has created a good team ethos with a culture of support, cooperation and debate usually manages meetings well. There is an element of the chicken and the egg in this, however, as it is often well managed meetings that have contributed to a positive team spirit in the first place.

Sometimes it is beneficial to have a facilitator rather than a chairperson, depending on the purpose of the meeting. If the aim of the meeting is to generate ideas or problem solve then a facilitator should be used. There are good reasons for the team leader not acting as facilitator and for a more neutral colleague to perform the role instead. It is almost impossible to run a fair, non-manipulative meeting when you have a personal investment in the subject matter. It is extremely difficult objectively to lead a group that is considering whether or not to discontinue an approach that you introduced and have faith in, for example. Even if you try not to influence the group your body language is likely to reinforce those who hold the same views as you. Quite unintentionally, you might end up dominating the floor in your role as chairperson. A possible solution is to invite a fellow middle manager with no preferences regarding outcomes of the meeting to act as a facilitator.

The facilitator needs to operate differently from a chairperson. They must be a neutral servant of the group and should not contribute or evaluate ideas. However, like a chairperson they must encourage all participants, protect individuals from personal attack and help the group arrive at a consensus. Facilitators make use of the following techniques to achieve their aims:

- using flip charts for recording ideas;
- brainstorming;
- boomeranging questions back to group members;
- taking 'straw polls' to see if a line is worth pursuing;
- using 'negative voting' to see what options cannot be lived with;
- sub-dividing the group for discussions;
- using open questions;
- using rounds to hear what everyone thinks.

Some thoughts on rooms and seating

The arrangement of seats and tables sets the stage for a meeting and can influence what will happen. A circular pattern encourages a sense of warmth and togetherness. It is easy to make direct eye contact with everyone else and there is a sense of equality from the chairperson not being the focus of attention. The circle can be useful for informal discussions. However, whatever the mood of the group it will be heightened by the circle. If anger or aggression is in the air, this negative energy will be aimed directly at individuals and can lead to heavy encounters. If the pattern is an oval, one person's energy is focused on the person opposite and is thereby critically restricted.

When everyone faces towards the person at the end of the table the collective energy is aimed at one individual, which is not conducive to problem solving but is fine for a formal information giving session.

One of the most effective ways to get a group to focus on a task is to seat the participants in a semicircle facing the question written on a flip chart and facing the facilitator. The energy of the group is now directed towards the common problem. Ideally, the semicircle should face away from the entrance to the room so that people coming in or leaving don't disrupt the flow of the meeting. The semicircle is ideal for presentations and problem solving sessions.

Most staff meetings take place in the staff room but it is important to consider whether this room is always the most *fit for purpose*. It would seem to make sense to hold subject meetings in an area where access to materials and resources associated with the subject is easy. For Key Stage, paired year group and year group meetings it is a good idea to locate the meeting in the classrooms of team members, in turn. This allows each teacher in the team the opportunity to show colleagues how their room is organised and to spend time talking about the children's work and displays. This is an important feature of schools aiming to create a collaborative climate. By holding meetings in the classrooms of team members, teachers have opportunities to learn from one another and middle managers can gain insights into what each team member is doing. Allowing teachers to talk about aspects of their work can also be very good for morale. The praise of colleagues can be a real tonic and therefore creating situations where this is likely to occur is a positive thing to do. There is much evidence that in successful schools teachers focus on and talk about teaching and learning; thinking carefully about where to hold meetings can encourage and focus this talk.

Reasons why meetings are unproductive

There are a number of common problems encountered in all kinds of meetings. Some of these can be solved by effective preparation and chairing, but others will be remedied only by building the kind of team culture that has been encouraged throughout this book. The following list covers many of these common problems:
- Everyone going off in different directions at the same time.
- Attacks on individuals rather than their ideas.
- People finding it difficult to join the flow and participate.
- Confusion over who is doing what in the meeting.
- Abuse of power by chairperson to achieve personal objectives.

- Too much information given in too short a time.
- Going over the same old arguments again and again.
- Lack of commitment from members, complacency or negativity.
- Lack of clarity over objectives.
- Hidden agendas.
- Problem avoidance – 'everything's fine'.
- People not listening to what is being said or only hearing what they want to hear.
- Poor meeting environment – people can't hear, can't see, are too cold or too hot.
- Lack of openness and trust.

Problem people

Some meetings are ineffective or have a negative feel because of the behaviour of particular individuals. Tight chairing will solve many problems but if certain people are persistently difficult it becomes necessary for the team leader to consider strategies for dealing with them individually. All participants of meetings display, at various times and in varying degrees, some of the following negative behaviour:

- Arriving late and stopping the meeting in order to catch up.
- Leaving early and disrupting the flow of the meeting.
- Popping in and out of a meeting to receive messages and phone calls.
- Having only one thing to say and constantly repeating it.
- Constantly putting new ideas down – 'that will never work'.
- Using non-verbal communication which is very dramatic – headshaking, rolling eyes, madly scribbling notes.
- Contributing nothing and appearing totally uninterested or, worse still, engaging in a separate activity such as reading a book or marking.
- Constantly whispering to a neighbour.
- Talking too much and dominating a meeting.
- Launching personal attacks on group members or the chairperson.
- Interrupting what people are saying and rephrasing things for them.
- Introducing gossip, anecdotes or rumours into a discussion.
- Using status, qualifications or length of service to argue a point.
- Telling the chair how to run the meeting.

It is important to think about how to deal with colleagues who are too shy to contribute in meetings, those who dominate meetings and those who are immature and distract others during meetings. Some basic tips are provided below.

Silent and shy colleagues

They can be encouraged by having their achievements recognised. This builds self-esteem. The team leader should try and bring shy persons into discussions, perhaps by asking for comments on areas that are one of their strengths. Any contributions made during meetings should be rewarded with positive words and encouraging body language. As their confidence grows ask them to prepare a contribution on a topic that interests them and is relevant and provide feedback afterwards, in private of course. Sometimes discussion can be improved by sub-dividing a group and asking smaller clusters of people or pairs to report back to the whole group. A pair of shy people could be put together at these times. If a leader is deeply concerned by a person's lack of participation this should be discussed with them in private but done with sensitivity so that the shy person does not feel guilty about their lack of involvement.

Dominant and self-opinionated colleagues

They can be given specific tasks to do that will prevent them dominating. Taking minutes is the obvious example. The use of sub-groups during discussions could allow dominant people to be clustered together. Essentially, though, over-bearing people need to be handled well by the chairperson who should insist on contributions being made through him or her and be assertive when self-opinionated people are dominating the meeting. This does not mean using put-downs but involves politely thanking them for their input and immediately bringing other people into the discussion before the dominant person continues with an argument or starts on a new point. Ultimately, encouraging everyone in a team to contribute and be assertive is the way forward. If dominant people are also aggressive, managers need to discuss their behaviour with them in private.

Colleagues who 'clown around' and distract others

Such people exist in some teams. They have a tendency to make light of serious issues by whispering to other colleagues or making inappropriate jokes. It is important to arrange seats in such a way that

whispering becomes difficult and small groups cannot separate themselves from the main body. Analyse your reactions to the clowning to see if you are making the situation worse and reward positive contributions with praise. If necessary, establish ground rules for the conduct of meetings with the whole team and confront bad behaviour publicly. If it becomes necessary to address the behaviour through a private meeting do ensure that there is plenty of praise for the positive things this colleague contributes to the team.

It is worth remembering that bad behaviour in meetings is unusual and that managers who have cultivated a collaborative, open and positive culture rarely encounter difficulties in meetings. If team leaders feel the dynamics in a meeting are unproductive then it may be helpful to invite a trusted outside observer to watch a meeting and provide feedback that the whole team considers together with a view to improving matters.

Reviewing your team meetings

Good managers reflect on all aspects of their practice. It is a good idea to find out from other team members what they think about the meetings you run. The Meeting Review Chart (Table 7.1) based on a design by James Sale (1998) could be used to provide feedback which

1	Agenda received in advance	1	2	3	4	5	6
2	Meeting in suitable environment	1	2	3	4	5	6
3	Meeting kept to time	1	2	3	4	5	6
4	Documentation available	1	2	3	4	5	6
5	Decisions taken	1	2	3	4	5	6
6	Action points agreed	1	2	3	4	5	6
7	Participation of all team members	1	2	3	4	5	6
8	Appropriate leadership style adopted	1	2	3	4	5	6
9	Minutes clear and useful	1	2	3	4	5	6
10	Planning and review integral	1	2	3	4	5	6

1 = poor, 6 = excellent

Table 7.1 Meeting review chart

could act as a basis for discussing meetings with others in the team and setting targets for improving meetings, if necessary.

Case study

Read the following comments and consider why the meeting in question was demotivating for this participant. Are there points here for middle managers as well as head teachers?

'Another staff meeting this evening . . . what a waste of time. Sue read out the agenda after everybody had arrived – the same old boring items. Why we have to sit and listen to her give a catalogue of things she has had to deal with this week I don't know. She always seems to assume that we want to know everything she's been doing; perhaps she wants us to know what she does for the extra money she gets for being head? I certainly get fed up of her moaning – I thought leaders were supposed to be positive and full of optimism!

The rules about snowy days are as they've always been, so why did we have to listen to them all over again? Surely Sue could have seen Karen, the new teacher, at some other time. She was asking so many questions that it wasted about ten minutes of the meeting.

I know I should take more interest but I'm really not that bothered about the details of building repairs. Can't they discuss that at governors' meetings? Nothing that was reported was really relevant to me (or the rest of the Year 5 teachers, come to think about it).

Target setting – that was an interesting item but we didn't really get a chance to discuss things fully. I don't see why the head and deputy should set targets for pupils without proper discussion with teachers. There'll be rumblings about this, I'm sure, but no one spoke out in the meeting.

To make matters worse the room was freezing, but nobody spoke up. You'd think Maggie, as deputy, would say something – enough people have complained to her about the heating going off so early. She spends all her time scribbling minutes and not joining in discussions, not that much real discussion takes place anyway. I wouldn't mind but we never see the minutes anyway. I suppose they are in the book if we really wanted to look.

Usha must be feeling really annoyed as a result of the meeting. It was so embarrassing when she was asked to brief us about the organisation for open day. It was obvious she wasn't expecting to speak to us about it. She did very well considering she had no notes with her. At the end of the meeting Sue asked if we could change next week's meeting to

Tuesday. I felt really angry – she knows how difficult it is for me to change child-minding arrangements. It wouldn't be so bad if meetings were productive! I felt very tense as I left for home. Never mind, while we were waiting for the head to arrive at the start of the meeting I did at least manage to chat to some of the teachers I don't usually have time to see.'

Reflection

This unfortunate teacher has a lot to feel annoyed about and it is not surprising she is feeling tense. Sue's handling of the meeting can be criticised on several grounds:
- An agenda was not provided in advance.
- The room was cold, and previous comments to Maggie seem to have been ignored.
- Usha had not been warned about having to speak.
- Irrelevant items were included – the head's work load and building issues.
- Time was wasted answering questions for a new colleague who could have been seen at a different time.
- A major issue – target setting – was glossed over with no opportunity for discussion.
- The time of a scheduled meeting was changed at short notice.

Apart from the head's failure to organise the meeting efficiently, communication in general seems to be poor, members of staff are not encouraged to assert themselves and there is certainly no culture of collaboration in evidence. However, colleagues were supportive and interested in what Usha had to say and they seem to cooperate with the head despite the shoddy treatment meted out by her. From this short extract we can conclude that the head lacks basic management skills and is failing to motivate, communicate and organise. Thankfully, there are probably few managers as incompetent as this head in real life!

Summary

Productive, well-chaired meetings can help to create a sense of purpose and greatly increase the effectiveness of teachers *as a team*. Equally, badly organised and poorly focused meetings lower morale and sap energy. There is a range of reasons for holding meetings and team leaders need to be clear about what the purpose of holding a meeting is and then adopt a style which suits that purpose. An amusing way of understanding what makes an effective meeting is to *consider what makes an ineffective meeting and then do the opposite!* These are a few suggestions:

1. Never create an agenda – people might think about the issues in advance.
2. Be late for meetings – keeping people waiting is a clear sign of your importance.
3. Never discuss one topic fully when you can confuse people with several.
4. Don't hurry decisions – if you wait long enough the problem might go away.
5. Don't have relevant papers to hand – you can all sit and wait for the photocopier.
6. Run long meetings and invite people for whom the issues are irrelevant.
7. Meet regularly when there is nothing to do.
8. Don't get things too clear, e.g. what has been decided – then you have a good reason for holding another meeting.
9. Don't set a finish time – people have nothing else to do and the head is sure to be impressed by the long hours your team puts in.
10. Take phone calls during the meeting – it shows how much in demand you are.

CHAPTER EIGHT

Administration and Resource Management

Introduction

Some aspects of middle management are less exciting than others but are nevertheless important in contributing to the successful running of a primary school. How well a school is organised vitally affects the lives of teachers and other employees and the education of the children. If administration and resource management are not efficient, stress and loss of morale will result. Indeed, even visionary and supportive team leaders will lose the respect of colleagues if their exciting ideas fail because of poor day-to-day organisation. It is not surprising, therefore, that the TTA includes the following competence in its document on *National Standards for Subject Leaders*: 'Subject leaders identify appropriate resources for the subject and ensure that they are used efficiently, effectively and safely' (TTA 1998).

Efficient administration has a lot to do with being a good time manager. Time management is addressed in Chapter 11 and the advice provided there should be seen as complementary to the tips given in this chapter. Resource management involves both day-to-day organisation of resources and planning for future resource needs linked to curriculum development. Chapter 9 addresses development issues and it is through development planning that future resource needs should be identified and budgeted for. Efficient administration and effective resource management both require highly developed organisational skills with thinking ahead being the key to success.

Administration

A glance at primary teachers' pigeon holes will reveal the tremendous amount of paperwork they have to deal with. However, most primary teachers receive very little or no non-contact time for all the administration they have to do. Even those who carry considerable management responsibility are likely to have heavy teaching loads. It is therefore vital to be clear about priorities. The administration and the paperwork should be seen as a *means to an end* not as an end in itself. Being an efficient administrator should help your team to provide top quality teaching and it is important not to lose sight of this. If you do then the pupils will begin to be seen as obstacles in the way of you doing your paperwork rather than as the clients who should be benefiting from any paperwork that you do.

Most administration falls into one of four categories:

1. Day-to-day tasks associated with your team's normal work. This includes such things as making sure the necessary teaching resources are available, dealing with work left by absent colleagues and making sure teacher assessed SAT marks are entered on record sheets.
2. Organising and administering your team's contribution to planned school events and activities. These might include organising SAT tests, report writing, open evenings, field trips and presentation evenings.
3. Preparing for OFSTED inspection.
4. Dealing with all the unanticipated paper that finds its way into your pigeon hole. Here, you are essentially reacting to things that come your way. These things often require a quick response. If you have planned in respect of the other three categories you will be able to respond to matters that occur in the fourth group more effectively.

It is important to be down to earth about administration. It has to be done and there are numerous practical ways in which you can help yourself to do it efficiently and effectively. Here are some useful tips:

- Your diary. Make sure all deadlines and commitments are recorded in your diary and then list them again as forthcoming items at suitable earlier points so that you are reminded of the need to get ready.
- Term/year planner. Take key events from your diary and locate them on a term or year planner so that you can see at a glance what is coming and where any bottle-necks might occur. Colleagues should have a copy of the planner so that they, too,

can organise their work in anticipation of known forthcoming events.

- Weekly planner. By putting items on to a weekly planning sheet you are able to prioritise between urgent and non-urgent jobs. Don't allow too many non-urgent jobs to go unattended to for week after week.
- Daily list. Have a list of jobs to do for each day. Ticking them off as you go along will give you a great sense of satisfaction. As new things crop up note them on your list; don't rely on your memory!
- Filing cabinet. Always file away important information and ruthlessly discard unimportant pieces of paper. Go through your filing cabinet once a term and remove information that is no longer relevant. An efficient filing system should allow you to find things in seconds rather than minutes and should be able to be easily understood by others. Should you fall ill colleagues will need to be able to lay their hands on papers that are normally your responsibility. Make sure your filing system enables them to do this.
- Computer. Use and develop your computer skills. Many aspects of administration can be made easier with a computer. Handbooks can easily be updated, class lists revised, pupils' marks stored efficiently and so on. If you use a home computer try and make sure it is compatible with your school system. Carry information on floppy disks so that you can work on files at home or at work but always remember to update information on both systems. Use file names which will not confuse you when you want to access information. Remember there is legislation concerning the holding of pupil information on computer so check out your school's policy with the senior member of staff responsible.
- Current folder. Hold documents that you are working on in a current folder. Items should not remain in the current folder for more than a couple of weeks.
- Highlighter. When you first read a document highlight key words and ideas. This will help you to process it much more quickly or to focus on the important parts if you have to return to it.
- Waste bin. A lot of what comes into your pigeon hole will be irrelevant. You will be able to tell very quickly if something is of no interest or is irrelevant. File such items in the bin. Do not become the kind of middle manager whose desk is covered with several piles of catalogues, circulars and out of date memos. A cluttered desk is usually a sign of poor decision making.

- The first hour of the working day. If your domestic arrangements allow, arrive at work in time to deal with routine administration. It is amazing how much you can get done before the pupils arrive. Teachers who arrive only a few minutes before the children often seem disorganised and look harassed. Feeling organised helps your performance. If you are unable to arrive early use your weekly planner to build in regular time slots for dealing with routine matters.

Managing resources

In the broadest sense the resources which have to be managed by team leaders include people, time, money and equipment/materials. Managing people has been addressed in earlier chapters and time management is considered in Chapter 11. The management of money and materials will be considered in this section. Money refers to the team's budget or *capitation* (the amount allocated from the school budget to your area for teaching equipment/materials). Teaching equipment/materials can include textbooks, stationery, paper, photocopies, videos, AV equipment, computers, software and more. Materials which need reordering yearly or termly because they are used up in the process of delivering the curriculum (for example, exercise books, paper, glue) are known as *consumables*.

Day-to-day resource management

Everyday in schools a wide range of equipment and materials are used. The ease and efficiency with which individual teachers are able to gain access to the resources they need can have a significant impact on their morale and on the learning of children in their care. A five-minute wait at the start of a lesson while a video and TV are located and set up is five minutes of learning time wasted; a lesson planned around a set of books which are then not available is likely to result in a very unproductive teaching session.

Team leaders must, therefore, devise a system for resource management that is both efficient and effective. A system will work only if it is adhered to by all colleagues. This is more likely to happen if colleagues have been involved in decisions about the system. Maverick behaviour should not be tolerated; individual teachers who hoard resources for themselves or hide sets of books should be challenged. Equally, teachers who forget to return resources or who do not look after sets of books should be gently reminded that they are inconveniencing their colleagues, even if unintentionally. Getting the team ethos right is important. If team members are respectful and supportive of one another and realise how their behaviour impacts on other colleagues (or, if they see colleagues as 'internal clients') then they are less likely to be uncooperative about making an agreed system for managing resources work. Of course, the team leader must set the tone and not abuse his or her position by always appearing to have the best classroom and resources.

It is not easy to advocate a particular system for resource management because all schools are very different in terms of buildings and organisation. A purpose-built school with good sized classrooms and adequate storage space will be able to organise things differently from a school with a number of 'temporary' buildings away from the main school. In some large primary schools AV equipment is held in a Resources Centre, in others year teams possess their own AV equipment and in very small schools all colleagues may share one TV, video, and CD player.

However, there are certain basic questions to ask when deciding on a storage system for the resources belonging to your team:

- How often will this resource be used? The more often it is used the more accessible it should be.
- Who needs to be able to use this resource? The more people who need access to a resource the more open its method of storage should be.
- For how long should we keep resources? Be ruthless about throwing out old resources. Storage space in most schools is limited and there is no point in keeping redundant resources in the hope that they might come in 'handy' one day.
- Who will be responsible for managing the storage of this resource? Remember, the team leader should not necessarily be responsible for all resources but all resources do need somebody to look after them.

When you have identified teaching resources which are regularly used by several team members questions need to be asked about possible locations:

- Can people get it without disturbing someone's lesson?
- Can it be reached without shifting other things?
- If sheets, are they kept in files, boxes or a filing cabinet?
- If books, can they easily be transported from room to room? Remember health and safety may be an issue here.
- If AV equipment, is the location secure and safe?

- Does the choice of location inconvenience some colleagues more than others?
- Who will keep track of resources? How?

Budgeting

Middle managers are likely to be responsible for spending a proportion of the school's budget. It is important that your share of the school's capitation is spent efficiently and in such a way that spending is related to your development plan, which in turn is designed to provide the best possible education for the children in your care. You will need to be able to account for the money you spend. There are three main elements to this task:

1. Linking the funds available to priorities identified in your development plan.
2. Keeping a record of the way money is spent and balancing the books.
3. Evaluating the effectiveness of your spending.

These elements are linked to the development planning process described in Chapter 9 and are illustrated in Figure 8.1.

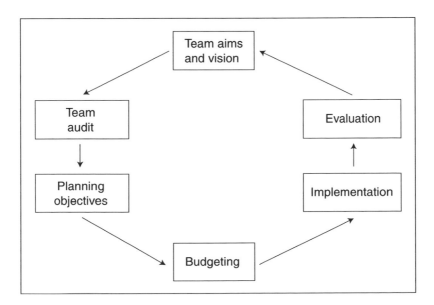

Figure 8.1 Linking development planning and budgeting

Gaining funds for development priorities

There is a chicken and egg situation with regard to linking funds to development priorities. Will your priorities be determined by the funds you know you will receive or should your priorities determine the funds you receive? There is no simple answer but most schools settle for a compromise. In small schools spending decisions relating to curriculum resources are likely to be decided through discussions involving all teachers. However, in very large primary schools a set amount of capitation may be provided to teams, determined by a figure per pupil being multiplied by the number of pupils taught by a particular team. There is usually a *weighting* included which means that practical subjects (which use more consumables) receive a higher figure per pupil. On top of this basic allowance, there may be a pot of money to bid for. This allows teams introducing new courses or approaches to present their case for additional funding. Money in most schools is very tight and so bids for additional money are only likely to succeed if the changes they finance meet one or more of the following criteria:

- the proposed change is a response to legislation;
- the proposed change is in line with the school's strategic plan and current development plan priorities;
- the proposed change is a response to market research findings (for example, carefully administered parent or pupil questionnaires);
- the proposed change will lead to measurable improvements in pupil performance;
- the proposed change is in response to the findings of inspection by OFSTED.

Clearly, a bid has to be professionally presented and realistic if it is to be taken seriously. The following points give an idea of the kind of information you should include in your bid for additional funds.

1. A rationale for your proposed change or spending. This will probably have emerged from the audit process (see Chapter 9).
2. How the proposal relates to school development plan priorities.
3. Clear objectives relating to your proposal.
4. An indication of how the effectiveness of the proposed spending might be measured. Can you produce hard targets? For example, if you want to spend on new books so that all pupils in Year 6 can take a book home do you expect an improvement in homework submission or SATs results? Can the improvements expected be quantified?

5. Very clear costings for materials, reprographics and INSET as appropriate. Can you show that you have 'shopped around' to get the best prices on materials and books?

Records of spending

As a middle manager it should not be necessary for you to keep detailed accounts. There will be a school administrator paid to do this. However, you need to keep track of your planned and actual spending during a financial year and also keep an accurate record of incomings and outgoings relating to school trips and the like. You may be required to produce such records for school auditors.

The easiest way to keep track of spending is to use an order book or file. Design a simple grid sheet using the following headings for columns:

- date (the date the order was placed);
- received (tick this column when items ordered have been received);
- details (include the supplier's name, catalogue reference number and brief description of the order);
- estimated cost;
- actual cost (as invoiced – this may include price changes, postage and packing etc.);
- balance (use pencil to write the balance based on estimated cost and then use pen to enter when actual cost is known).

As part of the development planning audit, include a financial review. Money is always scarce so it is worth discussing with colleagues how economies might be made. Here are some important questions to ask:

1. Can we save on exercise books and paper? In many schools paper is given out freely or pupils simply help themselves with the result that the paper bill becomes a significant part of the consumable resources budget.
2. Can we reduce expenditure on book replacement? In some schools there is a tremendous loss of books each year with a high cost attached. There is a big difference between having to replace old books and having to replace books because teachers have not kept accurate records of which pupils have borrowed them.
3. Can we reduce our photocopying bill? Photocopying is expensive and should be avoided except in emergencies or when only single copies of papers are needed. Some schools have less expensive reprographic facilities and colleagues should be organised enough to be able to take advantage of these and have worksheets

done in advance of a lesson. It is also poor use of a teacher's time to be standing at a photocopier.

4. Can we reduce our spending on consumables? Far too often items such as pencils and rulers are ordered year after year because pupils have lost or stolen them. While some loss is inevitable teachers should check that things are not going missing in their lessons. If all team members are determined to reduce the loss of consumables pupils will soon get the message.

Stock control

Coordinators of well run subjects know what resources are available to assist the teaching and learning process and make sure that colleagues also know what resources there are.

A stock book should be kept listing non-consumable resources for the subject, including serial numbers in the case of items of electrical equipment (useful if equipment is stolen or insurance claims have to be made). All books, slides, computer software and videotapes should be fully catalogued with reference to which Key Stage and year/topic they are appropriate for. Schemes of work should contain reference to key resources. Numbers of each set of books should be recorded and numbers checked at least once a term. Individual books within sets should be given a number. These numbers can then be entered into teachers' record books when books are lent out to pupils. In this way responsibility for looking after resources is passed to pupils. If books are lost parents should, as a rule, be charged the cost of a replacement. This helps to make pupils and their families take looking after books seriously.

Videotapes should be numbered so that they are easy to locate. If certain programmes are used regularly and the same video player is likely to be used note down the number displayed on the video counter and write it on the tape so that colleagues save time when trying to locate a programme. Just as considerate teachers clean the board they have used ready for the next teacher so rewinding a tape to the start of a programme is a helpful thing to do. Encourage colleagues to be helpful in this way. When a tape is full remove the tab so that it cannot be recorded over by accident. Have a booking system in operation for TV/video and other AV equipment so that colleagues are not planning lessons to include equipment that is unavailable.

Regarding consumables, it is likely that you will be ordering a similar amount of staple items such as exercise books and paper each year (unless significant economies can be made). Save a copy of each year's stationery order, so that you are not starting from scratch each time you put in an order.

Case studies

Outlined below are examples of how two primary middle managers manage their resources. Read the cases studies and then reflect on the advantages and disadvantages of each approach.

Study 1

Chris James, the English Co-ordinator in Oldton Primary School, had his own style of running the school library. He had an insatiable appetite for reading and he wanted all the children in the school to have a similar love of books. The library itself was managed by well meaning parents who had volunteered to come into school each afternoon, Monday to Friday. A rota system had been devised so that no one parent was involved in more than one afternoon library duty. Unfortunately there was no mechanism for ensuring that the rota system always worked. In theory, any parent unable to attend on their allotted afternoon had a duty to find a replacement but, in practice, this did not always occur. Consequently, some afternoons the library was devoid of a parent assistant. Chris was determined that if this situation arose it should not prevent classes using the library. Each class was allocated time in the library when books could be chosen or exchanged. The lending section of the library was controlled through a computer designated for the purpose and this was normally operated by the parent helper while the teacher dealt with behaviour and supporting the children in choosing their books. Most teachers made a written list of books borrowed and by whom so that the next time a parent helper was available the information could be entered in the computer. Unfortunately, this information was often misplaced or too hastily scribbled to make sense and therefore the computer could never be relied upon to give accurate data on all the books borrowed. It is hardly surprising that over a period of time the shelves in the library were sorely depleted. Despite the purchase of new stock each year, the library shelves never became 'full' of the reading material of which CJ was so fond.

Study 2

Denise Lindo is a Year 3 teacher responsible for music. For the non-specialist teachers in school she provides a system of song audiotapes and booklets containing the words to the songs, which she has put together over a number of years. These audiotapes and books are stored in plastic music chests, each one labelled with the correct year group number. Every teacher is allocated a time for using the materials, which are kept in Denise's storeroom. Teachers may send a pupil to collect the appropriate chest at an agreed time, e.g. before school or at lunchtime. The pupil is reminded that the chest must be returned by a certain time. Staff are made aware when the chest must be returned and that all items *must* be accounted for. A used tape must be rewound and repairs carried out on any damaged song books. Staff who return a chest late or have not carried out one or more of the necessary checks or routines are reminded by DL that they are letting the team down.

Reflection

Both subject leaders have their good points and bad points as do their approaches to the management of resources.

Clearly, Chris James is passionate about books and committed to giving pupils access to the library. He is willing to trust parent helpers and concerned not to alienate them by being rigid about the organisation of rotas. Unfortunately, his failure to ensure that the rota system is effective, and his inflexible view that classes should use the library regardless of the availablity of parent helpers, means that the very thing he feels so passionate about is under threat. It is a situation where the approach to the management of resources being taken is not fit for purpose and needs serious review. There is clearly much goodwill on the part of parents to be involved in the library. They might welcome a tighter system of managing things as something that would make their work easier. Through communicating the issues clearly to the helpers and inviting their suggestions for improving things, a way forward should not be too difficult to find. Chris has a clear vision for the library, but we can criticise him for not ensuring that management arrangements are appropriate for turning his vision into reality.

By contrast, Denise Lindo has a system that is tight but which requires all teachers to be as organised as Denise herself appears to be. Most teachers are probably more flexible and, even in these days of

National Curriculum, some sponteneity in the classroom is still possible. Unfortunately, given the tight rules and restrictions Denise has imposed, this sponteneity is unlikely to be in the area of music. Indeed, the way she has organised things means that non-specialist teachers may feel reluctant to get involved in music at all. It is unlikely that Denise will lose many resources because her system discourages colleagues from approaching her for help with music. This is a pity, as Denise has clearly worked hard to build up a body of resources suited to different age groups. Allowing colleagues to take resources into their area for a much longer period of time, while still holding them accountable for their eventual return, would seem a more sensible approach. Equally, if she made herself more approachable she could be a very valuable 'consultant' for music teaching across the school, a role she ought to be fulfilling. We can criticise Denise for allowing her rigid rules and pendantry to undermine any vision she might have for generating enthusiasm for music throughout the school.

Loss of resources is clearly an issue for all primary schools. However, resources are there to be used and a small amount of wastage is unavoidable. Sensible managers are able to create systems for managing resources which work, through discussing relevant resource issues with colleagues. Some degree of accountability placed on teachers is important, but systems that are rigid and bureaucratic are likely to alienate colleagues and be counter productive.

Summary

Some of the points made in this chapter may seem divorced from the vision creating and team building covered earlier in this book. They are actually closely connected. Good management is about being able to see the future and wider picture but also deal with the present and the nuts and bolts of day-to-day organisation. Of course, an *obsession* with the nuts and bolts is not healthy and may indicate that a team leader has got his or her priorities wrong. However, a middle manager who can help colleagues do a good job by having efficient systems for day-to-day organisation in place will gain much respect.

You will feel more organised if you are able to develop an approach to administration that is disciplined and does not allow paperwork to become the tail that wags the dog. Effective use of your diary and planner, ruthlessness over discarding much of the paper that appears in your pigeon-hole, and developing working patterns which include slots for attending to paperwork are all important strategies for dealing with administration.

The day-to-day running of your area will be enhanced if you are able to develop systems for the fair and efficient use of resources. Easy access to materials and books, an efficient booking system for TV and other equipment, and delegating responsibility for checking resources are all important. With regard to finance, ensuring that colleagues are committed to limiting photocopying, preventing loss of consumables and ensuring all books are accounted for will help to free up money for providing other things that team members feel are needed. This identification of needs should be linked to the development planning cycle and should involve all team members.

Finally, never lose sight of the fact that effective administration and resource management are not ends in themselves. They are important for helping you and your team to achieve the more important goals of providing a good education for your pupils and raising their levels of achievement. 'A meaningful life is not a matter of speed or efficiency. It's much more a matter of what you do and why you do it, than how fast you get it done' (Covey 1994). This observation should make just as much sense when applied to management in schools.

CHAPTER NINE

Managing Change and Development

Introduction

The current reform agenda for schools in England and Wales has had a profound impact on teachers in primary schools. The determination of successive governments to drive up pupil achievement and make schools more accountable has resulted in wave upon wave of centrally directed initiatives being implemented in schools. This 'top-down' approach to change has produced some improvements in those things which can easily be measured but, arguably, has created in some schools a kind of innovation fatigue and has left many teachers feeling de-skilled, mere technicians following the instructions of those on high.

Despite a heavily deterministic national agenda effective schools still feel that they can shape educational provision in their own way and can control change rather than be controlled by it. Such schools use the impetus of external reform to improve or develop themselves. Sometimes what they do is consistent with the national reform agenda, sometimes they introduce change because of particular circumstances unique to their situations. In these cases what is best for children in that school is always the driving force. Schools with the following features have been identified as most likely to manage change effectively:

- trust, openness and collaboration;
- clear underlying values and beliefs;
- good staff-pupil relationships.

Holly and Southworth (1989) see the culture of 'developing' schools as enabling, promoting learning and growth for adult members as well as pupils. They describe the culture as 'interactive and negotiative; creative and problem-solving; proactive and responsive; participative and collaborative; flexible and challenging; risk-taking and enterprising; evaluative and reflective; supportive and developmental' (Holly and Southworth 1989).

Change can be threatening and unsettling and can cause weariness and fatigue. Equally, introducing change can be an opportunity for learning, creativity and personal development. Effective management can make the difference between a cynical and lack-lustre approach to change and an approach characterised by enthusiasm and commitment. Middle managers play a vital role in the change process and their level of success in managing change will be dependent upon good interpersonal skills, a collaborative team culture and effective planning. The importance of middle managers in directing change is detailed under 'Strategic direction and development of the subject' on page 10 of *National Standards for Subject Leaders* (TTA 1998).

School development and the change process

It is important that managers understand how change affects the individual. All change causes a certain amount of stress to the individual but it will not necessarily always be negative stress. The extent to which a change is *desired* and *predicted* determines how stressful it will be. For example, taking up a new post can be stressful. This is because you are moving from what Plant (1987) calls 'firm ground' to 'swampy ground'. You are stepping out of a position where you feel confident, you understand the culture and your role is clear into an altogether more uncomfortable position where you are uncertain about your role, relationships and responsibilities. However, because the new job was desired and success in securing the post boosted your self-esteem you will probably turn the stress into creative energy and work very hard to make a success of the post.

There are other occasions where change that was not expected or desired can cause great stress and this, at least in the short term, can lead to loss of self-esteem, decline in performance and depression. It is clear from this that managers need to involve colleagues fully in decisions about change and the change process. Change should not be seen as undesirable or unexpected and the greater the involvement of team members in decisions about the future the less likely it is that change will have a negative effect on them. This is why a collaborative culture usually produces smooth and effective change.

Everyone has a need for a certain amount of stability, either personal or professional. The stress factors of moving house, getting married or divorced are well documented. A teacher experiencing stress outside work will be unlikely to embrace change in the workplace with enthusiasm. By recognising the need for some stability managers can show understanding and provide support. People come from different backgrounds with different experiences and therefore cope with change in different ways and at differing speeds. Managers need to acknowledge this when change is being introduced.

> When those who have the power to manipulate changes act as if they have only to explain, and, when their explanations are not at once accepted, shrug off opposition as ignorance or prejudice, they express a profound contempt for the meaning of lives other than their own. (Marris 1975)

Middle managers cannot control the speed of change that is centrally imposed but they can make the change less threatening by providing support for colleagues and by ensuring that the change is controlled, directed and shared. When a collaborative and supportive culture exists in a team, change can usually be accomplished smoothly. Indeed, in most successful schools bottom-up change is common, with discussion and the implementation of new ideas and ways of improving provision seen as quite normal.

Even so, change in schools ultimately concerns changes in individual practice, which some colleagues find more difficult to cope with than others do. It is likely that the implementation of a significant curriculum or organisational change will involve one or more of the following features:

- changes in the structure and organisation of the school; for example time-tabling or the shape of the school day;
- new or additional teaching materials; for example PCs in the classroom;
- teachers acquiring new knowledge, such as results from curriculum changes;
- teachers adopting new ways of working; for example moving away from a didactic style to resource based learning;
- changes in beliefs or values on the part of some teachers, the introduction of SATs or the introduction of setting, for example.

A fear of change or simply a desire to avoid the additional work generated by change can produce an initial reluctance to embrace a new idea from even the most dedicated teachers. In certain circumstances, though, opposition to change may be more pronounced. Hall and Oldroyd (1990) note that in settings where staff response to new initiatives is poor:

- morale is low;
- change agents are not respected;
- there is a track record of failed innovation;
- risk taking is discouraged;
- leaders are inflexible in their attitude;
- there is little outside support.

Managing development

Managing development in schools involves controlling and directing change in order to improve the service and nature of education provided. In turbulent times a clear sense of direction and routes to follow are essential and effective development planning should provide these. Development planning is now well established in just about all state schools with middle managers being actively involved in the process and critical to its success. According to Hargreaves and Hopkins (1991) the merits of development planning are:

1. It focuses attention on the aims of education.
2. It provides a coordinated approach to change.
3. It considers long term vision and short term goals.
4. It puts control of change into the hands of teachers.
5. Staff development becomes more focused.
6. The achievements of teachers in promoting change are recognised.
7. It becomes easier to report on the work of the school.

School planning involves thinking about long term and short term issues (see Figure 9.1) and thus schools should have (i) a strategic plan; (ii) a school development (or improvement) plan; (iii) Key Stage, year and subject plans; (iv) programme and policy plans; and (v) action plans. Together these plans help schools to provide answers to several important questions:

- Where are we now? (audit)
- Where do we want the school to be in five years' time? (vision)
- What changes do we need to make? (construction)
- How shall we manage these changes? (implementation)
- How shall we know whether our management of change has been successful? (evaluation)

Strategic plan

A strategic plan communicates decisions that have been agreed concerning the long term (usually three to five years) development of

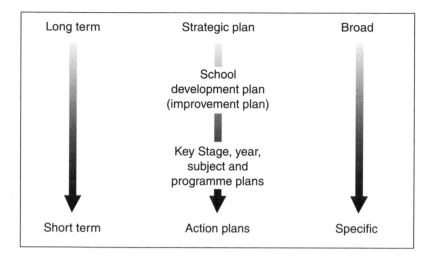

Figure 9.1 A hierarchy of school plans

the school. The strategic plan reflects the values, vision, mission, aims and policies of the school. These will shape the planning goals for the future.

Development (or improvement) plan

A school improvement plan prioritises a limited number of goals from the strategic plan. It contains a range of mandatory and discretionary goals. Typically, action points from OFSTED inspections form the basis for improvement plans but they are not driven exclusively by OFSTED. Internal audits and external market research might also shape a school improvement plan. According to Hopkins and MacGilchrist (1998) schools are increasingly using their development plans as a means of raising pupil achievement through focusing on the quality of teaching and learning. Improvement plans are often written in detail for the forthcoming year and in outline for the two following years. This three-year rolling plan approach helps to provide a balance between short and medium term planning.

Key Stage, year and subject plans

Key Stage, year and subject plans will be strongly influenced by the school's strategic plan, by school improvement plan priorities and by OFSTED inspection findings. However, teams may have areas for development that they themselves have identified and regard as important.

Programme and policy plans

Programme and policy plans may be written by small teams of people or by individuals. They are usually concerned with the implementation of inter-disciplinary programmes, possibly developed by working parties. Programme plans or policies on 'Staff Appraisal' or 'Recording and Reporting' are two examples.

Action plans

Action plans turn the first year of the development plan or programme plan/policy into a working document for teachers. Action plans describe and summarise what needs to be done to implement and evaluate key priorities. They clarify what has to be done by assigning responsibility for action. Action plans show:
- targets to be achieved in implementing a particular goal;
- resources allocated;
- individuals responsible;
- completion dates;
- success criteria.

The action plan is thus a convenient guide to action. The better the quality of the action plan, the more likely it is that implementation will proceed smoothly. The more effectively all team members can be involved in drawing up the action plan the more likely it is to succeed.

Making a success of team development/improvement planning

Middle managers can achieve smooth and successful change by creating a collaborative team culture in which individuals are constantly striving to improve the education they provide and by using well established development planning techniques. Team leaders operate within a wider school improvement planning context and so a clear understanding of the whole-school approach to development planning is important. The smaller the school, the easier it is to achieve a consistent whole-school approach.

The development/improvement planning cycle

Essentially, development/improvement planning is a cyclical process that involves audit, construction, implementation and evaluation. In many schools the audit and construction phases occur during the summer term and implementation usually takes place during the

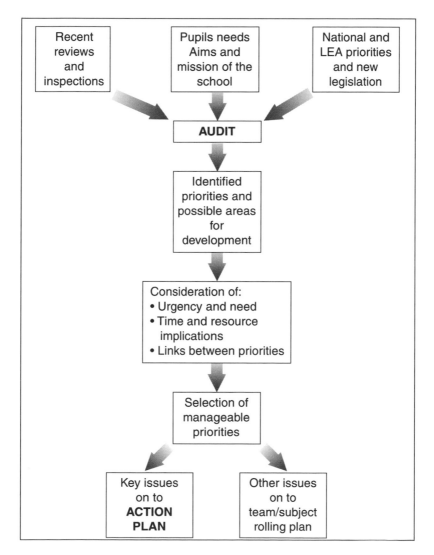

Figure 9.2 Construction of the team subject development plan

autumn and spring terms. Evaluation should be ongoing but with a more thorough evaluation at the end of the cycle, in the late spring term, which feeds into the audit. It is obviously the case that raising pupil achievement is a major aim, whatever the specific development/ improvement plan targets, and an analysis of SATs results should occur in July or September and be revisited at the audit stage of the cycle.

It is impossible to address all issues that might require attention in a development/improvement plan. Development/improvement planning involves making decisions about which issues take priority, which areas will be maintained and which will be developed. Highly successful schools and teams are likely to include more maintenance and fine-tuning than new initiatives in their development/ improvement plans. However, education operates in a rapidly changing world and it is unlikely that any team will ever be in a position where no change is necessary and no improvement is possible.

The audit

The audit stage is extremely important and involves a review of strengths and weaknesses. It provides a good opportunity for team building with openness, reflection and constructive criticism being essential. The audit should be seen as an evaluative summary of the school's performance in the key areas of its work. The key areas of its work should be defined in relation to pupil performance, national legislation and whole-school aims and mission. The audit should involve evidence gained from the evaluation stage of the development planning cycle and from other evidence available such as SATs results and the findings of OFSTED inspections.

It is also useful to think about conducting market research to assist with the audit process. Increasingly, parents' and pupils' opinions are being used to assist schools in making judgements about the quality of education that they provide. While some teachers are horrified by the idea of pupils assessing them, others are beginning to accept the notion of 'child as client'. Teams where openness exists and colleagues are supportive are more likely to consider using pupils' views as part of the evaluation and audit process. We often become aware through anecdotal evidence of what the views of pupils are but the picture we get is a partial one. Investigating pupils' attitudes in a more systematic way, therefore, would seem sensible, and the information gathered, if used sensitively, could help teams to consider how best to improve their practice. It could be used to inform decisions on curriculum and pedagogy and even for individual staff reviews and appraisals.

A subject or year group audit involves consideration of strengths and weaknesses of provision, but it isn't possible to conduct a *detailed* audit of every aspect of a team's work every year. A balance has to be reached between reviewing areas of provision which relate to whole-school development/improvement initiatives and reviewing aspects of provision because the team or team leader believes it is important to do so. Workload is a major consideration so there is a need to be realistic; attempting to do too much in any one year is likely to result in frustration if ambitious plans are not achieved.

The audit should involve answering such questions as:

• What are we doing well?
• What are we not happy with?
• What statutory requirements and LEA policies affect us?
• What are the constraints?
• What are the opportunities?
• What should we try and change over the next year?
• What should we try and change over the next three years?

Performance indicators

A performance indicator is a piece of information that helps you to know how well a person, group or an organisation is performing. It is important to include performance indicators in the audit process. SATs results and other assessment information such as reading age scores can be useful, especially when they are analysed to indicate 'value added'. Increasingly, schools are using sophisticated measures to establish how well they are performing compared with other schools catering for pupils of similar ability and backgrounds.

Quantitative performance indicators by themselves rarely provide definitive answers but they do help teams to focus on the important questions to ask. They draw attention to issues that deserve a closer look. Comparisons between one year and another, between subjects, and with local and national norms help to focus teams on the key question: are we doing the best we can for our pupils?

Middle managers must be committed to raising achievement in schools. The sensitive use of statistical information on pupil performance with teams and individuals can be a useful part of this process. However, if such performance indicators are used to blame and shame individual teachers it is likely that the collaborative and supportive culture that is so important for achieving success will be undermined. 'Total quality management does not seek to attribute blame, total quality management seeks to understand and control quality' (Smith 1996). Analysing pupil performance is likely to become increasingly important with the legal requirement (set out in DfEE Circular 11/98) for governing bodies to set targets for pupils' achievement in terms of the percentage of pupils gaining level 4 or above at the end of Key Stage 2, for example. It is also possible that in the future such information will be used to inform some kind of performance related pay scheme.

The development/improvement plan and the action plan

Once the audit has been conducted it is possible to translate the findings into a development/improvement plan or rolling plan and an action plan. Establishing priorities, and an order for dealing with them, is the way a team can control change rather than be controlled by it.

When choosing between priorities, in order to decide which issues should be dealt with urgently (action plan) and which should be addressed in the coming years the following questions are important.

1. **Urgency**
   - What is unavoidable (e.g. a legal requirement)?
   - What are the consequences of delay?
   - Will it wait or will things get worse?

2. **Manageability**
   - Can the development be achieved in a manageable time-scale or should tasks be sub-divided?
   - Have we got the resources to achieve the task?
   - Do we need outside support?

3. **Roots and branches**
   - Have we got the right philosophy, team structure and team skills to make the change work (the roots)?
   - Are the changes needed a natural extension of what we have already started (the branches)?

4. **Links**
   - Are priorities inter-related?
   - Will tackling one make it easier to address another?

Answering these questions will help a team arrive at an action plan. Action plans should capture long term vision in manageable short term goals. Action plans should set out specific success criteria, identify group and individual responsibilities and completion dates. Action plans state realistic targets to be achieved within a given time. Using a format such as the one provided in Table 9.1 helps to make action plan decisions easily accessible to team members and to senior managers and outside agencies.

When aiming to achieve complex objectives or where developments involve inter-related elements, it is important to undertake a critical path analysis. This involves agreeing a timetable for action and listing on it deadlines relevant to each stage of the proposed development. Summarising these on a grid which shows the months of the year, individual deadlines and who is responsible helps to improve the management of development.

Success criteria

Success criteria used in development planning should relate to specific targets. They should be capable of demonstrating that targets have been achieved. They should be used by teams during the review and audit stages of development/improvement planning, in order to evaluate success.

Of course, some success criteria will be more easily measured than others. If an objective is to rewrite a scheme of work then the new document will provide clear evidence that the target has been achieved. If a target is to increase the number of pupils at Key Stage 2 achieving level 4 or above in science then the percentage of pupils gaining level 4 compared with previous years might act as success criteria. However, in this case even if the SATs results seem to demonstrate success isolating cause and effect may be more difficult. In order to achieve better results more time may have been devoted to science; new schemes of work and classroom strategies may have been used; support may have been targeted specifically at borderline level 4 pupils and so on. Which of these initiatives (if any) resulted in the improvement will be difficult to establish. Indeed, changes in performance may be due to factors beyond your control, such as more able pupils, or may be due to subtle changes in the style of the SATs exam papers or teacher awareness of the style of the papers. This illustrates the difficulty involved in deciding on success criteria. It also warns us of the dangers of always seeking to demonstrate success in terms of only what is measurable in statistical terms.

Action Plan Summary Team/Subject _____ Date _____

Start date	Objective(s) Target(s)	Action needed	Person responsible	Assisted by	Resources, INSET and costs	Success criteria	Completion date

Table 9.1 Action plan summary sheet

Keeping developments on track

After the audit and construction stages of the development/ improvement planning cycle are complete it is important not to assume that agreed action will simply progress on auto-pilot. Successful implementation needs support and sustaining commitment is a key task for team leaders. The enthusiasm of even the most competent and committed teachers can wane simply because of the pressures of everyday teaching.

There are simple but effective ways in which middle managers can keep things on track. First, an occasional, informal enquiry about progress to a teacher demonstrates that their efforts are appreciated and provides them with an opportunity to raise with you any difficulties they are encountering. Second, having progress reviews built into some team meetings means that individuals with responsibility for action will have to report the progress they have made to colleagues. This helps to prevent complacency and again provides an opportunity for identifying difficulties being encountered. Third, an enlarged copy of the Development/Improvement Plan Summary should be displayed on a team notice board with targets achieved ticked or crossed out so that everyone has an idea of the progress being made.

If things are not proceeding to plan it is usually because time schedules are too tight, circumstances have changed, unexpected obstacles have been encountered or key colleagues have simply allowed matters to drift. Progress checks allow re-orientation to take place. Where a collaborative team culture exists, most problems can easily be overcome. If a major obstacle has emerged which the team was unaware of at the time of constructing the development plan it may be necessary to modify your targets. However, this should only be done if absolutely necessary.

Techniques for generating team involvement

Successful development planning depends to a great extent on staff commitment and involvement. Much of this book has been devoted to the effective management of individuals and teams and the creation of a positive collaborative culture. The audit stage of development/ improvement planning provides a great opportunity for a team to clarify its aims and philosophy and work together on deciding how the education you are providing can be improved. However, in a team where all members are not yet committed to the idea of continuous improvement, or where teachers are simply suffering innovation fatigue, generating interest in further development becomes a real challenge to middle managers. The key is to create opportunities for staff involvement so that they feel ownership of the development/ improvement plan. The imposition of change can never be as effective as the embracing of change.

Brainstorming is one way of generating involvement (see Chapter 5) and **process analysis** is another. This latter is a group problem-solving approach used for examining the operation of a process or procedure in order to identify ways in which it can be improved. 'Inducting' reception pupils and their parents, preparing Year 6 pupils for SATs and organising trips are all examples of *services* that might be improved by process analysis. The benefits of the technique are that it fosters collaboration, it increases commitment and it helps a team to develop a coherent view of a complex process.

The technique is similar to preparing a flow chart and involves the group in critical review by: mapping the main stages in the process; detailing what happens at each stage; evaluating each stage of the process; and agreeing strategies for improvement. Process analysis needs to be conducted in an atmosphere free from blame and where everyone's opinions are considered. The team should sit in a horseshoe shape facing a wall. Recording ideas on large sheets of paper on the wall means that the information is clear and all can see it. Diversions and side-tracking become obvious and are likely to be corrected by the group. Individuals can see easily how they contribute to the whole process under review. By increasing understanding greater collaboration during implementation can be achieved.

When auditing the work of a team a **SWOT analysis** should be conducted, involving all team members. SWOT stands for *strengths*, *weaknesses*, *opportunities* and *threats* and it is a useful technique for summing up the status of your subject, area or team in both a school and a national context. It helps a team to look to the future and avoid complacency. The team leader must prepare for the analysis by producing key questions that raise awareness of school and national issues.

Reflection: evaluating the work of your team

A Team Review Survey is an excellent device for contributing to the review and audit stage of a team's development/improvement planning cycle. A possible survey is provided as Table 9.2.

The survey should be completed and handed in confidentially.

Relative personal priority (A)		Reflects this team (B)	
1 = Top priority	4 = Not really important	1 = Strongly agree	4 = Slightly disagree
2 = High priority	5 = Low priority	2 = Agree	5 = Disagree
3 = Fairly important	6 = Lowest priority	3 = Slightly agree	6 = Strongly disagree

Number	Criterion	A	B
1	Schemes of work are agreed by the team as a whole		
2	Tasks are delegated fairly		
3	The team is receptive to new ideas		
4	Individual pupil records are detailed and frequently updated		
5	Schemes of work give detailed and clear guidance		
6	Opportunities are made for career development through appropriate delegation		
7	The team shows selectivity when considering innovations		
8	The team keeps abreast of recent developments in teaching		
9	Marking is consistent and adheres to clear criteria		
10	The content of schemes of work is periodically reviewed		
11	Designated roles in the team play to the strengths of individuals		
12	Resources are well deployed and targeted on priorities		
13	Pupils are given clear explanations of how marks are arrived at		
14	The schemes of work detail a range of teaching and learning styles		
15	The team is united in its attitude towards all key policies		
16	Resources are well organised and arranged		
17	Teachers are involved in making decisions on key issues		
18	The team has a sense of 'group spirit'		
19	There is an effective procedure for pupil self-assessment		
20	Pupil records are used effectively to monitor the progress of individuals		
21	Effective use is made of in-class support for special needs		
22	Teachers in the team support one another		
23	SAT results are analysed thoroughly to assist in raising achievement		
24	Able pupils are stretched and challenged		
25	Interpersonal relationships in the team contribute to effective team work		
26	Pupils are well prepared for SATs		
27	You feel able to raise issues that you feel strongly about		
28	The team has a clear sense of where it is going		
29	There are procedures for the moderation of assessments related to NC levels		
30	Team meetings feature developmental as well as administrative tasks		
31	Opportunities are created for colleagues to share good practice		
32	Effective support is provided in the team when behaviour problems occur		
33	Clear priorities for development are identified and adhered to		
34	Pupils' achievements are celebrated		
35	Day-to-day routine tasks are efficiently organised		
36	The team integrates with the main body of teaching staff		
37	Staff achievement is celebrated		
38	Pupil achievement is rewarded		
39	Pupils' work is well displayed		
40	The work of the team is effectively promoted		

Table 9.2 Team review survey

Participants should be encouraged to use the whole range of scores available and not restrict themselves to 3s and 4s. When all the sheets are returned the scores can be averaged to produce two rankings: one on the basis of 'importance' (column A) and one on the basis of 'performance' (column B). Each descriptor can then be placed into one of four categories:

1. **Those high in both importance and performance rankings.** These areas of success can be celebrated and analysed to see if the reasons for success can be replicated in other areas.
2. **Those high in importance but low in performance.** These issues will need to be considered for inclusion in the development/ improvement plan.
3. **Those low in importance but high in performance.** These issues might be unpopular 'housekeeping' tasks or irritating time wasters. It is important to consider which is the case.
4. **Those low in both importance and performance.** These can probably be ignored.

Summary

'The purpose of development/improvement planning is to improve the quality of teaching and learning in a school through successful management of innovation and change' (Hargreaves and Hopkins 1991). Middle managers are critical to the success of school development. By being systematic in their approach to development planning they can help to reduce the stress associated with change and can ensure that the aims and mission of a school are translated into practice through 'a logical progression from policy formulation to policy implementation within the planning hierarchy' (Giles 1997).

Middle managers will principally be involved in the writing of development/improvement plans and action plans for their areas. These form part of the School Development/Improvement Plan and contain targets relating to whole-school aims as well as targets generated by the team relating to issues of concern that they have identified.

Development/improvement planning is a cyclical process involving audit, construction, implementation and evaluation. It involves planning for the maintenance of aspects of provision which are effective as well as planning to tackle areas of weakness. It is important that planned developments are realistic and achievable, that people know clearly who is responsible, that clear time-scales are agreed and that success criteria are established at the planning stage.

Collaboration, openness and critical reflection are essential when teams are evaluating their performance. Collective ownership of the development/improvement plan with key tasks shared between team members is important for effective implementation. Team leaders need regularly to review progress so as to avoid developments falling behind agreed schedules.

CHAPTER TEN

Performance Management

Introduction

When it comes to the formal evaluation of the performance of colleagues many middle managers seem to get cold feet, despite making informal judgements about members of their team day in and day out. Yet evaluating performance of self and others is a key aspect of middle management. In future, the most successful individuals and schools are likely to be those who are the most effective learners. In a supportive culture individuals should be able to see that, ultimately, the pupils gain from the evaluation of teachers, because the purpose of the exercise is to improve teaching and thus pupil performance. With a national agenda for improving performance in schools some politicians would like to see appraisal formally linked to teachers' pay and promotion.

Autumn 2000 witnessed the start of a statutory system of Performance Management. On 1 September 2000 'new' regulations were introduced to replace the Appraisal Regulations of 1991. Although all the discussion surrounding the new regulations was about Performance Management (PM), surprisingly there was no mention of PM in the title which read: 'The Education (School Teacher Appraisal) (England) Regulations 2000'. Although the title may not appear to herald any change in approach, in actual fact it disguised a complete shift in culture. Instead of the old bottom-up appraisal approach of the 1990s, the new regulations outlined a top-down appraisal system for the start of the new millennium. Head teachers were told they had a statutory duty to ensure that:

- the process was implemented and managed;
- an annual report was provided for the governing body of the school;

- s/he was to act as a team leader to all or some of the staff;
- s/he underwent an annual review of her/his own performance.

The critical bullet point as far as middle managers in primary schools are concerned is that appertaining to 'team leader'. In small primary schools it could well be that the head decides to be 'team leader' to all staff. This could make sense in schools with other teaching staff numbering up to five. Beyond that number the workload could become onerous and at the same time could prevent members of middle management in school from developing an important facet of their role.

There is no doubt that if a system of appraisal is to succeed it must be accepted by all those involved as a rigorous and developmental process. It must also be manageable in that sufficient time is available for middle managers to demonstrate to the staff they are appraising that it is a worthwhile process and that they intend it to be rigorous in a positive, supportive and developmental way.

It is important, therefore, that the school's policy on Performance Management was arrived at through a consensual approach thus allowing it to become embedded in the school's team culture and collaborative approach to change. This should ensure that the conditions for improvement can be established and that they are linked to continuous learning and development.

Performance management – planning, monitoring and reviewing

Within the Performance Management cycle there are three stages which are likely to take place during a 12 month period – planning, monitoring, and reviewing – and all three will involve middle management if they are team leaders.

Planning

This stage involves the setting of individual teacher objectives within the context of the school's Development Plan. These objectives can in theory be between three and six in number (with three or four being a realistic number) and must contain one objective related to each of the following:

- pupil progress;
- improving the teacher's own professional practice;
- whole-school improvement.

It is likely that each teacher will have three objectives in mind at the start of each Performance Management cycle and certainly middle managers who are team leaders should be encouraging teachers to 'self-evaluate' prior to the objective setting meeting. The art of supporting teachers in their objective setting will, however, come to the fore *during* the meeting. The team leader will need to know the teacher, and his or her strengths and weaknesses, and have relevant statistical data on the pupils in the teacher's class, in order to negotiate manageable, yet challenging, objectives.

The middle manager acting as team leader must ensure that the right climate for negotiation is established. Neither participant must feel they need to rush through the business. Sufficient time, therefore, must be set aside, free from outside interruptions and pressures. The atmosphere needs to be friendly but business-like where the emphasis is on making the right decisions for the teacher, the children they teach and the school within which they work. At the end of the meeting the teacher must feel *ownership* of the objectives and see them as challenging yet realistic. The team leader must also feel that the objectives are challenging but realistic, and should have a sense of satisfaction at having played an important part in this first stage of the PM process.

Monitoring

The monitoring element of the PM process may seem an overwhelming prospect to a middle manager who has not previously been involved in such a task. Although training will not provide the complete answer, it should take place before a middle manager is asked to undertake the role as team leader. The task itself should then be broken down into manageable parts. Planning is where all good lessons start and having a clear idea of how the teacher tackles this aspect of teaching provides a 'sketch' of what classroom practice is like. Ideally the lesson/curriculum planning should be looked at by the team leader and the teacher together. Next the team leader should seek evidence of 'outcomes' in the classroom by looking at classroom displays, exercise books and test results. Talking to pupils during observed lessons and for a short time at the end usually helps to support or confirm the other outcome evidence.

Watching a lesson taken by the teacher is the part which has to be most carefully planned by the team leader, again in conjunction with the teacher. The objectives for the observation must be agreed in advance in order that the teacher knows and understands what is happening and does not see the team leader as a threat. Using a generic observation form as a template, the foci for the observation should be discussed and agreed. Some people use observation forms which can be found in teacher union information packs on Performance Management. Many schools have designed their own observation forms based on their experiences of monitoring literacy and numeracy lessons. There should also be a number of 'ground rules' agreed upon before the team leader observes a lesson. It must be clear how they are going to record: for example, in a formal manner – seated with a clipboard with no interaction with the pupils; or informally – moving around and chatting (when appropriate) with the pupils, teacher and support staff. Will they see *all* the lesson, or the start and part of the middle before popping back before the end? In all cases the team leader must make a point of thanking the teacher when they leave the classroom at the end. Feedback from the lesson should preferably be in two forms: 'instant' verbal feedback within 24 hours (ideally at the end of a teaching session, i.e. morning session – lunchtime feedback; afternoon session – after school feedback); and written feedback within five to seven working days. Part of the 'ground rules' discussion should be that 'feedback' meeting times are agreed. Team leaders will have their own ideas about how much written feedback is required but thought should be given to the volume of paperwork generated by the PM system. Bullet point statements could help reduce the volume where the rule of thumb is five positive statements to two developmental statements.

Oral feedback
This potentially is the most difficult part of monitoring, since it is the time when the teacher is at her or his most vulnerable. Tackled with care and sensitivity it could prove to be the most rewarding time within the PM cycle but inversely it could prove to be the most problematic and damaging. The emphasis must be on the positive in order to prevent loss of esteem and morale. Even in the worst case scenario, it is unlikely every aspect of the lesson was a disaster and therefore the team leader must ensure that the observation form has a number of starred positives to feed back. The areas for development can be raised for discussion by the team leader but it has to be remembered that there must still be room for negotiation.

Skills needed for effective feedback are:
- managing/controlling the meeting;
- seeting the ground rules;
- establishing rapport;
- questioning skills;
- ability to paraphrase/synthesise;

- ability to reflect;
- ability to challenge;
- ability to summarise;
- ability to draw conclusions;
- ability to listen.

The team leader will also be required to observe the school's agreed code on confidentiality following all meetings.

Although the foci of the lesson to be observed will be agreed in advance the criteria used by OFSTED inspectors for judging the quality of teaching can provide a useful framework for observation and discussion. The Inspection Schedule requires inspectors to base their judgements on the extent to which teachers:

- have a secure knowledge and understanding of the subject they teach;
- set high expectations to challenge pupils and add to their knowledge and understanding;
- plan effectively;
- use methods which match lesson objectives and the needs of all pupils;
- manage pupils well and achieve effective discipline;
- use time and resources effectively;
- assess pupils' work and use assessment to inform planning.

Reviewing

The middle manager in the role of team leader will also be required to measure the degree of progress made against the set objectives. Hopefully, throughout the year, the teacher being evaluated will have had this meeting in mind and will have reached her or his goals. The timing of the meeting may be crucial in that it could occur at the end of the school year when the teacher is tired, jaded and certainly ready for a rest. A better time (if it is line with the school's PM policy) could be the autumn term prior to the new planning meeting and the setting of fresh objectives.

If the agreed objectives have not been met then this could be the time when the middle manager is forced to grasp one or more nettles, but preparation for this eventuality needs to be made in advance. Knee-jerk reactions on the day of the review meeting should be avoided. The process has to be supportive and developmental, hence careful thought needs to be given to the most suitable type or form of training which may be required.

But ideally the end of year review will be a time when the team leader can celebrate with the teacher the success of achieving the set objectives. The team leader too should experience some satisfaction in knowing that they have contributed to improving matters in a positive way for the member of their team, the pupils they teach and the school within which they both work. No mean feat!

Objective setting

Performance Management objectives are likely to be formulated in the first instance by the teacher but it also likely that the team leader will need to work on ensuring that these are appropriate. The objective may be there in essence but require some re-wording. Criteria for a good objective are that it should be:
- clear;
- concise;
- measurable;
- challenging – but realistic and achievable;
- not set in concrete – it may need to be adjusted to accommodate a changed situation.

The use of ambiguous language to describe objectives should be avoided with the teacher and the team leader clear what exactly is meant. The emphasis needs to be on making the objectives 'measurable' and 'challenging'. If the objective is difficult to measure then the question should be asked - is it worthwhile? If the objective appears 'soft' then there is a danger we could slip back into an appraisal system similar to that of the 1990s, which was considered 'too cosy' by the DfEE. The Performance Management top-down process, in which team leaders have a large part to play, is expected to prevent this situation reccurring.

Case study

Kim Adara is a young teacher with five years' experience of working in Key Stage 1 and lower Key Stage 2. At present she is in charge of a Year 3 class with additional responsibility for music across the school. She leads a choir, comprising mainly KS2 girls which she trains two lunchtimes a week. Her lack of free time, she argues, prevents her monitoring how music is taught across the school and therefore she is not in a position to report how well, or otherwise, it is being taught. Kim relies heavily on the professionalism of her colleagues to follow the curriculum guidelines on music which she wrote some three years ago. She enjoys teaching her own class but is having some difficulty with a group of boys who at the end of KS1 had disappointing SATs results which indicated they were operating below their potential, and whose behaviour was 'challenging'.

Self-evaluation prior to meeting her team leader led her to write down the following 'possible' objectives for discussion:

1. Rewriting the music guidelines.
2. Organising a system of monitoring music across the school.
3. Monitoring the progress of the boys in her class.

As a middle manager team leader you are presented with these objectives at your first PM planning meeting. Should they be accepted as they are? Do they need to be changed? If yes, how do you go about tackling the changes?

The objectives suggested by Kim Adara do meet the DfEE demands in that one is related to pupil progress, another to improving her own professional practice and a third connected with whole-school improvement. However, they cannot be accepted as they are: they meet few of the listed criteria for a good objective (see above). They are concise but crucially they are not measurable. Pointing this out to Kim Adara should provide the starting point for negotiations, which in turn will hopefully result in meaningful objectives being agreed. Her revised objectives may, for example, be:

1. Rewrite music guidelines by _____ (date). Presentation of the draft document to the staff by _____ (date). Final version of the 'new' music guidelines to all staff by _____ (date) with a review date of _____ (date) attached.
2. Organise a music monitoring week during the second half of the spring term this academic year (exact time to be negotiated with Senior Management). During the week teaching staff to provide copies of their music planning. One class in each year group to be visited, to observe a music lesson (to be negotiated with class teachers). A short questionnaire to be completed by Years 5 and 6 pupils in connection with music.
3. All children to be assessed using the Qualifications and Curriculum Authority (QCA) optional tests at the end of the first and second terms and again at the end of June. The parents of the under-achieving boys to be invited in to discuss the school's concerns and to suggest a programme of additional help including homework, individual targets and sanctions for poor behaviour. Statement of targets to be written down and agreed with the pupils concerned.

Using pupil performance data

There are increasing amounts of quantitative data available on pupil and school performance, available to managers in primary schools. The school may have its own internal testing procedures, particularly in connection with reading, spelling and mental calculations. Some information may be shared with the LEA, e.g. NFER reading scores. Many schools use the full range of optional SATs in addition to the compulsory Foundation Stage baseline assessments and the end of KS1 and KS2 SATs. Most LEAs now provide their schools with information that allows them to compare their performance with that of other schools in the immediate area and with the whole LEA. The DfEE provides comparative data twice a year for schools through the spring Performance and Assessment Report (PANDA) and the 'autumn package'. All this information should be available to middle managers should they require it and some of it can be very useful, although the art of using such data is to be selective.

The 'big picture' information provided by the DfEE allows senior management to check their school's position against those described as 'similar' and against all schools across the country. This data may prove useful when 'marketing' the school and may provide an indicator of whether OFSTED will be carrying out a full or short inspection the next time they visit. Information which can be gathered at school level and which at first glance appears to indicate that one teacher is obtaining better results than another should be handled with care. Comparing the results of tests in one teacher's class with another will only be meaningful if you are certain that all groups contain pupils of similar ability and that the pupils all began the year with a similar level of knowledge and understanding.

Testing all Year 5 children, for example, at the start of the academic year could provide some useful data. Once a pupil has a 'baseline test' score it is possible to compare their subsequent test scores with pupils who had the same baseline test scores. In this way a 'value-added' figure can be arrived at. This is a better way of comparing the performance of one teacher's pupils with another, though it is still very dangerous to jump to conclusions on the basis of small numbers of pupils. The use of such data to identify particular pupils who appear to be under-performing in order to target them for support would, of course, be good practice. Schools need to ensure that teams analyse value-added data together in order to look for trends and evidence of good practice boosting results. If one teacher, for example, seemed to be successful in helping the very able to make exceptional progress then that teacher's methods would be worth sharing with other colleagues.

This approach still has its limitations. Even when there is clear evidence of value added it is not clear whether you are adding greater value than other schools dealing with pupils of similar ability. This is where evidence from sources such as Durham University's value-added information system, headed by Professor Carol Fitz-Gibbon, becomes useful. The system for primary schools, known as PIPS (Performance Indicators in Primary Schools), monitors the progress made by individual pupils, including their self-esteem and the quality of life within the school, between Reception and Year 8. By looking at the results for each child, it is possible to see how pupils taught by member of staff X have performed compared with pupils taught by member of staff Y.

The important difference between this data and raw performance data is that it comes much closer to comparing like with like. With this information it is not possible for a colleague to explain away poor pupil performance with excuses like 'my group was weaker', 'children always do less well in this particular subject because it is harder' or 'the results are good for the children in our school'. Clearly, small numbers of pupils will still limit the validity of conclusions reached from the data but there is no doubt that the PIPS information helps middle managers to ask the right questions about the achievement of pupils taught by teachers in their team. Used sensitively, the data can help colleagues in a team become more reflective and analytical and can help to pinpoint areas of excellent performance as well as areas of concern. Where excellent value added is in evidence praising the teacher concerned and sharing the good practice that produced the results are essential.

Dealing with incompetent teachers

Once Performance Management is established in schools it is likely that middle manager team leaders will become increasingly accountable for under-performance in their team. With the current emphasis on target setting and the wealth of statistical information now available on pupil achievement this trend is likely to increase. Middle managers must, therefore, establish the nature of the under-performance and devise strategies to raise standards and develop the skills of under-performing team members. Fortunately, inspection evidence shows that most teachers are competent or better and there is advice provided in Chapter 4 on how to get the best out of such colleagues. In the case of teachers faced with incompetence allegations, the Teaching Competence Project, directed by Ted Wragg at the University of Exeter, found that about a quarter of them were able to improve their performance. Effective support and the teachers' desire to improve were key factors in these successes.

When judging a teacher's competence it is important not to act purely on first impressions, anecdotes or information provided by others. There are many different styles of teaching and you should not jump to conclusions about a teacher's competence simply because their style of teaching is idiosyncratic. If there is clear evidence of under-performance based on a significant amount of pupil achievement data or if repeated negative comments about a teacher are being made then you need to investigate. Evidence needs to be gathered from a variety of sources including observation of lessons, inspection of children's work, lesson plans, pupil course evaluations and pupil performance data. In well managed teams these forms of evidence already form part of regular discussions and any under-achievement is likely to be out in the open anyway.

If you feel that there is indeed under-performance, your initial strategy must be one of support. Try coaching first, but if there is no improvement then the colleague must be informed of your concerns. These must be clearly expressed and you must try and temper specific criticism with praise for what is going well, wherever possible. The initial interview should be minuted and should provide opportunities for the under-performer to respond and provide an explanation or express a viewpoint. Objectives should be set, with a time limit for their achievement and a date for review. These should be realistic and challenging and the time-scale manageable, generally within a term.

Under-performance in the classroom can result from teachers simply becoming complacent or may be because they failed to develop basic classroom management strategies during their early years of teaching. It is very rare for teachers to be incompetent in all aspects of their work and context can be very important. Teachers sometimes cope well with some groups but not others; successful teachers in some schools may flounder when they move to a school with a very different intake of pupils. Assistance must be offered to enable under-performers to improve. Some additional training may be necessary and it might be appropriate for another colleague to assume a mentoring role rather than the middle manager. In some circumstances, under-performance may be caused by factors outside school such as domestic problems. Such situations may be temporary and, with your support, the problem could soon be resolved. However, it is important to put the needs of the pupils first. Personal problems may be a reason for under-performance but not a justification. Sympathy and support are vital but if you and senior colleagues allow very poor performance to continue for several terms or even years you are failing in your duty as managers. According to Maureen Cooper, writing for governors:

> Sometimes the downward slide has gone on for some time before any formal efforts have been made by management to improve the situation. You could say that in this situation you've got two failures to deal with: not only the under-performing teacher but also the failure of management to deal with the problem early enough.

(Cooper 1998)

Senior managers must be kept informed of the objectives you have agreed and if these objectives are not met a review meeting must move matters forward. Discuss the implications of the meeting with the appropriate senior member of staff. If you have supported and praised while at the same time been clear about the areas that need to be improved you have acted reasonably. There is no 'quick-fix' for under-performing teachers and in the end it may be that competency procedures have to be initiated. This will be the responsibility of the head teacher and senior members of staff but it is important that you have done all you can to help your colleague improve before this point. If competency proceedings are started you will, of course, be involved and you need to seek advice from your union. You will need to keep detailed records of all meetings and targets. Competency proceedings can be stressful both for the colleague concerned and their team leader. Whatever the justice of your case it is likely that the teacher concerned will feel defensive and betrayed. The ethos of the team will almost certainly be affected. You must, therefore, be certain that a member of staff is under-performing and that this under-performance is detrimental to the pupils and to your team before proceedings commence.

Summary

Middle managers who are formally involved in evaluating the performance of colleagues must work hard to create the kind of open and supportive culture which makes Performance Management a natural and unthreatening feature of the organisation. Spreading good practice and enabling colleagues to improve aspects of their work are necessary if pupil performance is to be improved.

There is now a wealth of data available relating to the performance of pupils. The use of this data is important for evaluating a school's performance and the performance of teachers. It can influence setting future School Improvement Plans, the Curriculum Coordinator's targets, and it may also be helpful in the process of Performance Management regarding the objectives set by teachers being evaluated, if used with caution.

While acknowledging there are very few incompetent teachers, if a middle manager has evidence that a colleague is seriously under-performing then it is important to grasp the nettle by putting in place a programme of support. At the same time, objectives to help the member of staff to improve should be set. In extreme circumstances it may be necessary to consider competency procedures or dismissal. This will be a matter for the head teacher and senior managers to handle but it is vital that you work closely with them, adhere to procedures and keep accurate records of all meetings with the colleague concerned.

CHAPTER ELEVEN

Stress Management and Time Management

Introduction

It is necessary in a book on middle management to consider the management of stress since the pressures and demands on middle managers are such that some potential for stress almost inevitably goes with the territory. School middle managers and teachers are not the only people who have to deal with stress; many would argue that stress is endemic to modern working life and that understanding the causes of stress and strategies for dealing with it are therefore essential life-skills. Managers have a responsibility to be aware of when they are stressed themselves and of when those they manage are stressed. In their approach to team relationships managers can greatly reduce the stress felt by others, and by managing their own stress appropriately they can make themselves more efficient, more effective and more self-fulfilled.

Many people feel that lack of time to do jobs properly is a major cause of stress and, because of the perceived link between time and stress, time management is also considered in this chapter. Being able to organise time effectively is essential for all managers; those who are unable to do this will find that work encroaches further and further into their evenings, weekends and holidays and, except in the case of workaholics, this in itself will become a major source of stress. The good news is that there are some surprisingly simple techniques for improving time management and, while some people seem to be *naturally* better at managing time than others, everyone can improve their time management if they are determined to do so.

Some thoughts on stress

According to the Education Service Advisory Committee (1992) stress at work is 'a process that can occur when there is a mismatch between the perceived pressures of the work situation and the individual's ability to cope with it'. David Fontana (1989) defined stress as 'a demand made upon the adaptive capacities of the mind and body. If these capacities can handle the demand and enjoy the stimulation involved, then stress is welcome and helpful. If they can't and find the demand debilitating, then stress is unwelcome and unhelpful'. This definition is useful for several reasons. First, it reminds us that stress can be both good and bad. Second, it isn't so much pressure that determines whether we're stressed or not, it is our reactions to it. Third, if our body's capacities are good enough, we respond well to stress, if they aren't we give way. Typically, too little pressure results in boredom and frustration; a moderate level of pressure is stimulating and actually improves performance; whereas too much pressure becomes debilitating and reduces performance (Figure 11.1).

Each individual has a different capacity for dealing with pressure and so a task that causes little anxiety for one person may cause considerable anxiety for another. Much depends on the individual's personality, experience and motivation, as well as support received

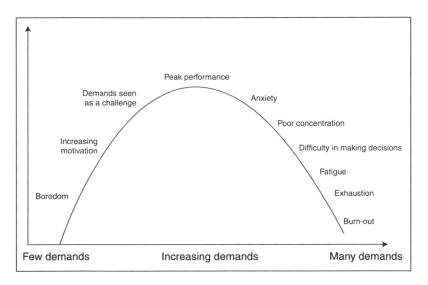

Figure 11.1 The effect of increasing pressure on performance at work

from colleagues and managers, as to how they will react to a potentially stressful situation. In addition the experiences that people are encountering outside the workplace are significant. A stressful domestic situation coupled with pressure in the workplace could produce an intolerable level of stress for some people. It is important, therefore, that managers encourage a collaborative and open culture in which colleagues are willing to talk about stressful situations they face and in which people support one another. An effective manager should be able to gauge the level of pressure needed for the most effective performance of each team member. A newly qualified teacher may be finding the behaviour of a particular class stressful whereas an experienced colleague may be undergoing the stress of marital separation, which is having an impact on their working life. Clearly, there are ways in which an effective manager could provide support in order to help both colleagues. This would be likely to generate respect and appreciation and to be repaid with goodwill in the future.

Causes of stress

It is generally acknowledged that death of a spouse, divorce, marital separation, death of a close family member and pregnancy are all causes of stress. These events are clearly outside the control of middle managers, though being aware of them happening in the lives of team members and responding with sensitivity is important. Across a wide range of jobs the following are regularly mentioned as causes of stress: nature of supervision, relationships with supervisor, relationships with peers, working conditions, salary, status and job insecurity. Some of these are outside the control of middle managers in schools but some can be much affected by them. Relationships feature strongly as causes of stress, which underlines the importance of creating the positive relationships and empowering culture advocated throughout this book.

Questionnaires used by Peter Fleming with teachers over a period of time have included a section on the causes of stress. While not claiming any reliability for the results, it is interesting that the same causes are always listed. These include:
- heavy workload;
- constant change;
- not enough time to do things thoroughly;
- OFSTED inspections;

- being unable to satisfy the conflicting and increasing demands of parents, pupils and managers;
- negative media coverage of education;
- lack of respect from society;
- lack of recognition for skills;
- increasing accountability but decreasing professional freedom;
- not knowing how colleagues rate you;
- not feeling valued for all the time devoted to the job.

According to Gold and Evans (1998) 'an unresolved mismatch between a personal philosophy of education and the organisation's educational philosophy' is also a potential source of stress. This, and many of the points made above, can be directly influenced by middle managers. Productive relationships and a collaborative team culture are essential for minimising stress. Recognising skills, increasing autonomy, involvement in decision making, providing effective feedback on performance and praising commitment are all things that have been encouraged in this book. Middle managers can also influence workload, and how change is managed and response to OFSTED inspections.

According to the National Association of Head Teachers, increased illness among teachers who go through OFSTED inspection is not uncommon. In a survey of 1,220 head teachers, forty per cent said staff illness increased in the three months following inspection. One possible explanation for this, provided by Elaine Williams (1999), is that teachers are unable to separate work and personal identity. Teaching is so personal that when OFSTED comes into a school teachers feel that they are being assessed rather than their teaching. If they are criticised they can begin to feel worthless as *individuals*. Likewise, if they are praised their self-esteem is boosted and they feel good about *themselves*, not just their teaching.

Good middle managers help to minimise the stress of an inspection by ensuring that their house is in order. Good teams have a positive ethos, clear goals, well designed schemes of work, good monitoring procedures and effective teaching. With these things in place there is little to fear from inspection. Confident middle managers are proud of their team's achievements and will want to help inspectors to see their area at its best by being proactive from the start. If middle managers have confidence in their team and are relaxed about inspection because they know all is well they will be helping team members to feel confident and in control. But if a year leader or subject consultant is not effective, if confidence is unjustified because all is not well, or if there is a panic leading up to inspection to put things right, it will not be easy for team members to feel in control and confident. In these circumstances stress is much more likely and the ineffective middle manager must accept a major part of the responsibility for this.

Identifying stress

Someone suffering stress may exhibit some or all of the following symptoms:
- a general deterioration in performance at work;
- an increase in sickness absence, which may fall into a particular pattern of frequent short periods of absence, possibly due to stress symptoms such as headaches, difficulty breathing, poor sleep patterns, indigestion and palpitations;
- an increase in irritability resulting in conflict and tension with other colleagues and a deterioration in relationships;
- loss of motivation and job satisfaction;
- less contact with people outside work;
- in some cases, over eating and/or an increase in alcohol consumption.

If stress is not tackled it can result in high blood pressure, heart disease, anxiety, depression, ulcers and thyroid disorders.

Controlling the stress of team members

The responsibility for the creation of a safe place of work lies with the employer but it is down to senior and middle managers to enact this responsibility. Sound management can prevent teachers and other employees becoming over-stressed in several ways.
- The school and team culture should ensure that stress is not seen as a weakness in the individual and that employees suffering stress will receive support without being made to feel guilty.
- The job itself must be manageable and the person's abilities, skills and experience must match the requirements for the job.
- Stress often occurs during periods of change. Team involvement in planning and managing change will go a long way towards reducing its negative impacts.
- Training must be provided to assist teachers in meeting the demands of change.
- Effective communication must exist so teachers have an accurate perception of the role they have to perform.

These points need also to be considered by senior managers in relation to their handling of middle managers.

Controlling your own stress

Psychologists identify certain individuals as being more stress prone than others. They are usually people who have high expectations of themselves, are very task and result orientated, tend to work quickly and find inefficiency in others frustrating. It is much harder for such people to control stress than other personality types, but not impossible. Recognising your potential for stress and being proactive in controlling stress are both important. If stress really is endemic to modern working environments then it is necessary to anticipate it and develop strategies that will prevent it rather than waiting until you feel stressed and then considering what you ought to do about it. Some pointers for minimising stress are:

1. Get your time management right (see below). This will make you much more effective in all aspects of your job.
2. Maintain a sense of humour. Take what you do seriously but don't take yourself too seriously. Teachers should be able to laugh at themselves, and if you cultivate humour as part of the team culture this will be a real antidote to the pressure of the job.
3. Remain optimistic. If you focus on the negative you will soon get yourself on a downward spiral. Always think positive, and recognise the progress made rather than dwelling on the distance still to go. Hackneyed as the phrase may be, try to see your glass as half full rather than half empty.
4. Have a life beyond work. It is essential that you engage in activities away from school. A successful family life and satisfying social life make you a more interesting and rounded person. Too many late nights at the word processor or too many working weekends build tension and resentment. It is in everybody's best interests that you remain healthy and positive, knowing when to 'draw the line' with work is important. There may be some evenings and weekends when it is impossible to avoid school work but an effective manager does not need to be on the job twenty-four hours a day.
5. Some managers arrive at school an hour before the school day begins and work on until 5.00 or 5.30 p.m. and then take no work home. While this wouldn't suit everybody it is one way of clearly demarcating working life and home life which can help you to 'switch off' once you leave the school buildings.
6. Learn not to take things personally. Managers must be able to cope with healthy debate and argument and not be distressed if things do not always go according to plan. A good team is one

that allows discussion and diversity of views and managers need not feel threatened by this.

7. Exercise. Obviously, your age will determine the kind of exercise that you can perform but everyone should engage in some form of regular exercise as a means of reducing stress through the release of endorphins.

8. Taking up a new post can be stressful but it is also true that staying in one job for too long can become a cause of stress for some people. With a new job there is much excitement and challenge; you are trying to prove yourself and often don't notice or resent the hours you are putting in because of the satisfaction you are deriving. Once you have been in post a few years devoting long hours to what have become routine tasks rather than challenges can become a source of irritation. If this is the way you feel then it might be time to think about a job move; motivating others becomes difficult if you are no longer motivated yourself.

Some thoughts on time management

The principles and skills of time management are as relevant to teachers and managers in education as they are to managers in other walks of life. In an ever more demanding and stressful profession effective time management is vital for survival. Far too many middle managers find themselves *living to work* rather than *working to live*; a situation that is not sustainable in the long run and which can cause burn-out and serious health problems. Many teachers devote very long hours to their work out of genuine commitment and a desire to do the best for the children they teach. While this is admirable in one sense, *expecting* teachers to devote every evening and weekend to their jobs in order to maintain the nation's education system is not acceptable and is a recipe for stress-related illnesses and marriage breakdowns among teachers.

Effective teachers and managers learn to use time efficiently. It is revealing to discover that those complaining the most in staff rooms about lack of time are often very inefficient in their own use of time. Likewise, teachers who are actively involved in extra-curricular activities and award bearing INSET are often also the members of staff who can be relied upon to get a job done efficiently. Indeed, it is likely that they also have fulfilling family lives and an active social life. Some people seem to be *naturally* good time managers and this is reflected in all areas of their lives. Even so, there are strategies which everybody can use to become better time managers.

How is effective time management achieved?

There is a difference between doing a job effectively and doing a job efficiently. Effectiveness means doing a job to the required standard whereas efficiency involves doing it in the right way and at the right time. Good time management helps people to increase their efficiency and maintain or improve their effectiveness. In recent years teachers have had to cope with increases in work load and the only certainty about the future is that change in education will continue as more and more is expected of our schools. Being effective and efficient in such a climate is essential. Working smarter not harder is the way to survive and this requires a systematic approach to work and to life in general.

According to Wood (1991) there are three characteristics of effective time managers which he calls the 'three Ts':

1. **Thought.** They achieve their goals by thinking about what they have to do, questioning its value and prioritising.
2. **Technique.** They plan when and how they will undertake each task so as to optimise their use of time.
3. **Temperament.** They try not to panic when new tasks come along because they realise that worrying wastes time and solves nothing. Likewise, when things go wrong they do not spend hours thinking 'if only I had . . .'. Instead, they conduct a review of why things went wrong and then plan to ensure that the same mistakes are not made in the future.

Planning, prioritising and deadlines

There is a cliché that suggests that if we fail to plan then we plan to fail. All effective middle managers need to plan so that they can spread their work load and prioritise. Making effective use of a planner/diary is essential and some practical tips on this are provided in Chapter 8 in the section on Administration.

Covey (1994) suggests a variation on planning by use of a Time Management Matrix (Table 11.1). All tasks should fit into one of these categories. Obviously, the urgent and important matters require your immediate attention. Items in the other boxes must be dealt with in order of priority. At the bottom of the scale non-urgent and unimportant tasks should probably be crossed off your list altogether. It is useful to try and predict the amount of time needed for each

	Urgent	Not urgent
Important	• Crises • Pressing problems • Deadline driven projects, meetings	• Preparation • Prevention • Planning • Values, clarification • Relationship building • Empowerment
Not important	• Interruptions, some phone calls • Some mail, some reports • Some meetings • Many pressing matters • Many popular activities	• Trivia • Junk mail • Some phone calls • Time wasters • 'Escape' activities

Table 11.1 Covey's time management matrix

activity before hand. Bear in mind, though, that initially it is more likely that you will underestimate the time required than overestimate it. With practice you will become more accurate, and the knowledge gained will prove invaluable for future planning.

Setting deadlines for the activities on your list is a good way of focusing the mind and avoiding 'drift', which results in important but not urgent tasks never being tackled. Deadlines for all tasks must be realistic and you should avoid setting deadlines that result in you putting off tasks until the day before they have to be completed. 'Working to the wire' is a bad habit and one that you should plan to avoid. It allows no further time to reschedule the work should a crisis arise. Set your own target date for completing each task some time in advance of the school deadline. This provides a safety net should a crisis arise. Encourage this practice in your team by negotiating deadlines for work you need from them which give some flexibility in case of illness or absence. Encourage a total quality management approach so team members see one another and see you as 'internal clients'. If deadlines are missed then someone is being let down and put under pressure, which is not fair. A supportive and empowering team ethos does not mean being sloppy about deadlines. If these are negotiated then everyone should adhere to them.

Delegation

If management is the art of getting things done through people then delegation is essential to good management. Most middle managers spend time doing things which should or could be done by someone else. Delegation should not be abdication but, used properly, is a feature of effective team work and staff development. As we saw in Chapter 4 delegating needs to be used in conjunction with supporting, coaching and directing in order to get the best out of team members. In Chapter 5 we considered an effective team to be one that used the strengths of each team player by delegating tasks appropriately. Where there is a gap between the current ability of a person to carry out a task and their potential ability, it is well worth spending time instructing them. Staff training is a good investment in the future, when team members will be able to complete tasks with decreasing levels of supervision. It can be tempting to try to do everything yourself because it seems quicker, for fear of being outshone by a colleague or simply because you feel you are paid to do more. However, fair and effective delegation is a must for middle managers and should be cultivated as a key feature of supportive teamwork.

Making decisions and being assertive

Procrastination can be a great time waster. While it is a mistake to make snap decisions before you have all the necessary information, dithering between choice A and choice B will not make the eventual judgement any more correct. Managers must be able to weigh up the facts and make decisions, even if they don't always get them right! Another form of procrastination is continually putting off jobs you don't like doing. Competent time managers identify the tasks they least like doing and use strategies to help them overcome their natural reticence to do them. Strategies include:
- setting deadlines for completion of unpopular tasks;
- breaking tasks down into manageable stages;
- tackling difficult jobs early in the day when you are fresh;
- rewarding yourself for finishing a task;
- getting a colleague to check that you have done the work.

When it comes to paperwork procrastination must be avoided. There are three options with paperwork: deal with it straight away; deal with it later; or put it in the bin. It is essential that junk mail is put straight in the bin. Correspondence and memos that can be dealt with quickly should be attended to on the day they arrive in your pigeon-hole. Paperwork that will require more serious attention should be listed in your planner as a job to be dealt with. Try not to let paper pile up on your desk. Use your filing system to save you time. Make good use of technology also. Handbooks, class lists, letters to parents, exam papers, schemes of work, worksheets etc. should all be stored on disc so that they can be modified easily rather than completely rewritten.

Assertiveness is another essential ingredient in good time management. There are occasions when even the most caring manager needs to complete an urgent and important task and so does not welcome interruption. If you are respected by colleagues and provide support and encouragement, setting aside some time when you don't want them to interrupt you should not be seen as unreasonable. Likewise, if one of your team is in the middle of an urgent task then you should not expect them to drop everything in order to discuss some less important matter with you.

Sometimes middle managers feel under pressure because of tasks with unrealistic deadlines set by the head teacher. It is important for middle managers *as a group* to be strong if they are presented with unreasonable requests from the head teacher. When asked individually to undertake a task it can be difficult to refuse because you don't want to offend senior colleagues or appear uncooperative or lazy. However, by taking on too many new tasks, aspects of your existing work might begin to suffer and so you need to learn how to say no without offending. The art of saying no diplomatically lies not so much in what you say but in the way you say it. Speak with confidence, be honest and say what you feel in a controlled way. Try not to allow your emotions to be demonstrated. Never be sarcastic or aggressive. Nor should you apologise profusely or put yourself down. Sometimes a compromise rather than a refusal is possible. Some tactful phrases you could use are:

- I feel honoured that you have asked me but . . .
- Yes, but it will have to wait until after . . .
- Yes, but I couldn't finish it by . . . because I have . . . to do.
- I would be happy to do that but let me know which you would like me to do first as I already have . . . to do.
- It would be possible but if I devote time to . . . I won't be able to do . . . so which would you prefer?

Note that effective time management does not mean saying no to everything. It is one of many strategies, not a quick-fix solution to your workload, and indeed if used to excess there is a danger that others will see you as uncooperative. A collegiate 'can do' culture cannot be created by people who say no to everything but, equally, hard working and competent managers and teachers should not feel guilty if they occasionally say no, especially to requests likely to impact negatively on existing areas of their work.

Self-assessment and reflection

Are you a stress-prone person?

Below are some questions to help you identify how stress-prone you or your colleagues are. They are based on a questionnaire provided by Cooper and Sutherland (1997). Give yourself or your colleague a score on a 1–11 scale for the bi-polar statements provided. The first one has the scale included so you can see where low and high scores fall.

1. Casual about appointments 1 2 3 4 5 6 7 8 9 10 11 Never late
2. Not competetive — Very competitive
3. Good listener — Anticipates what others are going to say (attempts to finish for them)
4. Never feels rushed, even when under pressure — Always rushed
5. Can wait patiently — Impatient while waiting
6. Takes things one at a time — Tries to do many things at once
7. Slow, deliberate talker — Fast and forceful speaker
8. Cares about satisfying him/herself no matter what others may think — Wants a good job recognised by others
9. Slow doing things — Fast doing things (eating, walking, etc.)
10. Easy-going — Hard-driving, pushing him/herself and others
11. Expresses feelings — Hides feelings
12. Many outside interests — Few interests outside work/home
13. Unambitious — Ambitious
14. Casual — Eager to get things done

Reflection

The higher the score received on this questionnaire, the more firmly an individual can be classed as stress-prone. People who are highly stress-prone are often blind to their own behaviour. If you are scoring this questionnaire to assess your own personality and suspect that you are stress-prone it is likely that you will find it hard to be completely honest in your self-assessment. To get a more accurate assessment it is useful to ask someone who knows you well to complete the questionnaire based on their perceptions of your workplace behaviour.

Psychologists use the term 'Type A personality' for those who exhibit strong stress-prone tendencies. Such people can be difficult to work with. They display the following characteristics:

- devotion to work, working long hours and feeling guilty when not working;
- a chronic sense of time urgency;
- a tendency to schedule more and more into less and less time;
- a tendency to attempt to do two or more things at the same time;
- a dislike of being kept waiting, especially in queues;
- difficulty in talking about anything other than work;
- a strong need to be in control;
- a very competitive outlook.

It is their constant need to compete that can make Type A people difficult to work with. They tend not to be good listeners and like to keep strict control over what is going on. They often do jobs themselves rather than taking the time to show someone else what to do, so they fail to develop their staff and rarely delegate. They may expect everyone around them to work to their demanding pace and schedule, including long hours of working and skipping lunch breaks in order to meet unrealistic goals and deadlines. Ironically, Type A people are frequently rewarded with promotion because, in the short term at least, they manage to move things forward. But in the longer term Type A behaviour becomes dysfunctional for an organisation.

It is important that managers who recognise Type A behaviour in themselves consider what effect they might have on others in their team. Arguably, it is impossible to change personality but it is possible to modify some behaviour associated with personality. Reflective managers with Type A tendencies need to become aware of the potential dysfunctional effects of their competitiveness and drive and to acknowledge that their desire to control will not help to produce an effective and empowered team. Through knowledge comes strength, and with greater self-awareness Type A middle managers can modify their behaviour so that they maintain their sense of drive while using management techniques that are likely to produce effective and focused teams. The techniques required for this have been stressed throughout this book.

Summary

Too little pressure can result in boredom; a moderate level of pressure is stimulating; but too much pressure causes stress and thus reduces performance. An effective middle manager should know his or her team well and be able to judge the level of pressure needed to get the best performance out of each team member. An effective middle manager will protect the team from unnecessary stress by encouraging a supportive and open culture, and will manage his or her own stress by cultivating a positive outlook and develping a fulfilling life beyond school.

Stress management and time management are linked. By using time efficiently middle managers can increase their effectiveness and reduce stress. Considering what constitutes inefficient use of time and the thinking that goes with it can help to clarify the strategies that can be used to improve time management. Consider the following and then **do the opposite**:

- Don't invest in a planner and never have your diary to hand – you have a good memory and that should be enough!
- Don't bother with targets – team members might feel too pressured!
- Never prioritise the tasks you have to do – you work more efficiently when you suddenly realise the deadline is tomorrow!
- Don't make a daily list of things to do – if a task is really necessary someone will remind you it needs doing!
- Never delegate – you're paid to do more and team members have enough on with teaching!
- Never say no however unreasonable the request – senior management might think you lack commitment!
- Never reply to memos immediately – decisions are always better for being given plenty of thought!
- Allow people to interrupt you at all times – it shows you are a caring manager!
- Never throw junk mail straight in the bin – you need to consider whether it might come in handy one day!
- Each day and at weekends take as much paperwork home as you can manage to transfer from your desk to your briefcase – the more you have with you the more you are likely to do!
- Don't store class lists, letters to parents, schemes of work, handbooks, worksheets, test papers etc. on a word processor – you rewrite them every year anyway so what's the point?

Links to TTA Priorities for Middle Managers

Throughout this book reference has been made to *National Standards for Subject Leaders* (TTA 1998). Below is a list of skills and attributes mentioned in the document which the authors consider relevant to *all* middle managers, and the chapters in this book you will find relevant to each one.

Skills and attributes	Relevant chapters
a. Leadership skills – the ability to lead and manage people towards common goals. Team leaders should be able to:	
1 secure commitment to a clear aim and direction for the subject	2,3,4,6,7,9
2 prioritise, plan and organise	8,9,11
3 work as part of a team	5
4 deal sensitively with people, recognise individual needs and take account of these in securing a consistent team approach to raising achievement	4,5
5 acknowledge and utilise the experience, expertise and contribution of others	2,3,4,5
6 set standards and provide a role model for pupils and other staff	1,4,5
7 devolve responsibilities and delegate tasks, as appropriate	4,9
8 seek advice and support when necessary	10,11
9 command credibility through the discharge of their duties and use their expertise to influence others	4,5,6,7
10 make informed use of research and inspection findings	3,9,10

b. Decision-making skills – the ability to solve problems and make decisions.
Team leaders should be able to:

1	judge when to make decisions, when to consult with others, and when to defer to senior managers	4,5,6,7,10
2	analyse, understand and interpret relevant information and data	9,10
3	think creatively and imaginatively to anticipate and solve problems and identify opportunities	9

c. Communication skills – the ability to make points clearly and understand the views of others.
Team leaders should be able to:

1	communicate effectively, orally and in writing, with the head teacher, other staff, pupils, parents, governors, external agencies and the wider community	1,6,7
2	negotiate and consult effectively	4,5,6,10
3	ensure good communication with, and between, staff in your team	6,7,9
4	chair meetings effectively	7

d. Self-management – the ability to plan time effectively and to organise oneself well.
Team leaders should be able to:

1	prioritise and manage their own time effectively	11
2	achieve challenging professional goals	4,9,10
3	take responsibility for their own professional development	1,9,10

e. Attributes
Team leaders draw upon the attributes possessed and displayed by all successful and effective teachers in the context of their leadership and management roles including:

1	personal impact and presence	1,6,7
2	adaptability	3,5,9
3	energy, vigour and perseverance	1,4,5
4	self-confidence	6,7
5	enthusiasm	1,2,4
6	intellectual ability	10
7	reliability and integrity	1,2,3,4
8	commitment	1,9

References

Adair, J. (1997) *Leadership Skills.* London: IPD.

Ainscow, M. (1994) *Creating the Conditions for School Improvement.* London: David Fulton Publishers.

Belbin, R. M. (1981) *Management Teams: Why They Succeed or Fail.* London: Heinemann.

Belbin, R. M. (1993) T*eam Roles at Work.* Oxford: Butterworth-Heinemann.

Blanchard, K. (1994) *Leadership and the One Minute Manager.* London: Harper Collins.

Bush, T. (1994) 'Theory and Practice in Educational Management' in Bush, T. and West-Burnham, J. (eds), *The Principles of Educational Management.* Harlow: Longman.

Clarke, P. (1998) *Back from the Brink: transforming the Ridings School – and our children's education.* London: Metro Books.

Cooper, M. (1998) *The Right Time to Sack a Poor Performer.* TES, 9 October 1998.

Cooper, C. and Sutherland, V. (1997) *30 Minutes To Deal With Difficult People.* London: Kogan Page.

Covey, S. (1994) *First Things First: Coping with the ever increasing demands of the workplace.* London: Simon and Schuster.

Davies, B. and West-Burnham, J. (1997) *Reengineering and Total Quality in Schools.* London: Pitman.

DFE (1993) *Effective Management in Schools: A Report for the Department for Education via the School Management Task Force Professional Working Party.* London: HMSO.

DfEE (1998) *Teachers: Meeting the challenge of change.* London: DfEE.

DfEE (1998) *Target Setting in Schools.* Circular 11/98. London: DfEE.

Drucker, P. F. (1990) *Managing the Non-Profit Organisation: Practices and Principles.* London: HarperCollins.

Education Service Advisory Committee (1992) *Managing Occupational Stress: A Guide for Managers and Teachers in the School Sector.* London: HMSO.

Fontana, D. (1989) *Managing Stress.* London: Routledge.

Fullan, M. and Hargreaves, A. (1992) *What's Worth Fighting for in Your School?* Milton Keynes: Open University Press.

Giles, C. (1997) *School Development Planning: A practical guide to the strategic management process.* London: Northcote House.

Gold, A. and Evans, J. (1998) *Reflecting on School Management.* London: Falmer Press.

Hall, V. and Oldroyd, D. (1990) *Management Self development for Staff in Secondary Schools, Unit 2: Policy, Planning and Change.* Bristol: NDCEMP.

Handy, C. and Aitken, R. (1986) *Understanding Schools as Organisations.* Harmondsworth: Penguin.

Hardingham, A. (1985) *Working in Teams.* London: IPD.

Hargreaves, D. and Hopkins, D. (1991) *The Empowered School: The management and practice of development planning.* London: Cassell.

Holly, P and Southworth, G. (1989) *The Developing School.* London: Falmer.

Hopkins, D. and MacGilchrist, B. (1998) 'Development Planning for Pupil Achievement' in *School Leadership and Management* **18**(3) 409–24.

Lewis, P. (1975) *Organisational Communications.* Colombus, Ohio: Grid.

MacGregor, D. (1960) *The Human Side of Enterprise.* Maidenhead: McGraw-Hill.

Maddux, R. B. (1986) *Team Building.* London: Kogan Page.

Marris, P. (1975) *Loss and Change.* London: Anchor Press.

Marsh, J. (1992) *The Quality Tool Kit: An A-Z of Tools and Techniques.* New York: IFS International.

Maslow, A. H. (1970) *Motivation and Personality.* New York: Harper and Row.

Pacific Institute (1997) *Investment in Excellence: Personal Resource Manual.* Seattle: Pacific Institute.

Peters, T. (1991) *Beyond Hierarchy: Organisation in the 1990s.* New York: Alfred A. Knopf Inc.

Plant, R. (1987) *Managing Change and Making it Stick.* London: Fontana.

Riches, C. and Morgan, C. (1989) *Human Resource Management in Education.* Milton Keynes: Open University Press.

Sale, J. (1998) 'Keeping The Dynamism: Some basic tactics for avoiding stale meetings' in *Managing Schools Today,* September 1998.

Sallis, J. (1997) 'Studies on Change' in *Managing Schools Today,* September 1997.

Sammons, P. *et al.* (1995) *Key Characteristics of Effective Schools.* London: Institute of Education.

Sammons, P., Thomas, S. and Mortimore, P. (1997) *Forging Links: Effective Schools and Effective Departments.* London: Paul Chapman Publishing.

Smith, P. (1996) 'Tools For Measuring Quality Improvement' in *Management in Education* **10**(2), 5–7.

Teacher Training Agency (1998) *National Standards for Subject Leaders.* London: TTA.

Thomson, R. (1998) *People Management.* London: Orion.

Trethowan, D. M. (1991) *Managing With Appraisal.* London: Paul Chapman Publishing.

West, N. (1997) 'A framework for curriculum development, policy implementation and monitoring quality' in Preedy, M., Glatter, R., and Levocic, R. (eds) *Educational Management.* Philadelphia: Open University Press.

Williams, E. (1999) 'Ofsteditis' in *TES Friday.* 26 March 1999.

Wood, I. (1991) *Time Management in Teaching.* London: NEP.

Index